# A DISCIPLINED MIND AND CULTIVATED HEART

### AND

Frederic W. Lieber

AuthorHouse™
1663 Liberty Drive
Bloomington, IN 47403
www.authorhouse.com
Phone: 833-262-8899

Because of the dynamic nature of the Internet, any web addresses or links contained in this book may have changed
since publication and may no longer be valid. The views expressed in this work are solely those of the author and do
not necessarily reflect the views of the publisher, and the publisher hereby disclaims any responsibility for them.

Any people depicted in stock imagery provided by Getty Images are models,
and such images are being used for illustrative purposes only.
Certain stock imagery © Getty Images.

This book is printed on acid-free paper.

ISBN: 979-8-8230-1560-8 (sc)
ISBN: 979-8-8230-1562-2 (hc)
ISBN: 979-8-8230-1561-5 (e)

Library of Congress Control Number: 2023918963

Print information available on the last page.

Published by AuthorHouse  12/20/2023

**author**HOUSE®

# TABLE OF CONTENTS

# DEAN'S FOREWORD

In July 2020, when I was appointed to my current role as dean, I did not realize that in a few short years, we would be celebrating 100 years as a school. As I considered how best to celebrate our 100-year anniversary, writing a commemorative book seemed important. Yet the weight of our history left me wondering how far the IU libraries' archives could extend in documenting the school from our beginning to our current global reach and import to the state of Indiana. Of course, the archives are vast, and they inform this commemorative book.

Because the archives are indeed extensive, I knew it would take a talented writer and much support to research them, select those items that conveyed the breadth and depth of our school's history, and tell our story well. We also needed a writer who could look beyond the archives to other sources of historical information about the school. And we needed a writer who knows the school and would be willing to take on this project. Thanks to a suggestion from two faculty members, I invited Fritz Lieber to write the book, and even though he was writing another book, he responded quickly to say that he would be honored to document our school's history. That was December 2022, and he completed the draft of the book, as promised, by June 1, 2023.

As Fritz outlines in the Acknowledgments section of the book, so many people gave generously of their time to provide background information and editing suggestions. These people include current and emeriti faculty and deans and staff who could help fill in missing historical details. Dean Emeritus Don Warren took on an extensive role, serving as the book's primary editor and engaging in frequent exchanges with Fritz as he completed each chapter. I am deeply grateful to everyone who contributed to this book.

So much could be written about the last 100 years of the School of Education, but commemorative books should be celebratory and brief. There is much to celebrate. We proudly say "education changes lives," and over the past century that's countless lives changed. As we celebrate our 100th anniversary this year, I hope this book leaves you inspired by all that has been accomplished by the School of Education and hopeful for the future of education in the state of Indiana and beyond.

Anastasia (Stacy) Morrone
Dean, School of Education

# AUTHOR'S FOREWORD

If it is sad to begin a celebration with a regret, it would be sadder not to. My sole regret is that I cannot give life to all the voices of my school.

The history of the School of Education is so complex, so rich, I could not cite all the names or achievements, even all the struggles, of our great institution in this modest book. If your favorite staff member or director or professor is not here, blame me not history.

As I thumbed old pages in the archives and read about events or saw photographs of people I knew but had no room to cite, I heard myself sighing. This book is full of missing persons. The most I can hope for, if this history is successful, is to rely on others to honor the silences and complete the story with their finishing touches of memory and understanding. One silence was purposeful. Except for the dean, I did not name current faculty or staff. In my Acknowledgments I cited current employees and others, but not in my narrative.

My grandfather was a freshman at IU in 1914. As he and I walked through campus in his late 80s, he showed me two gingko trees under which he often studied. They still stand between Owen and Maxwell Hall across from Dunn Woods. I used to take my students to those magnificent trees, their beds of butter-yellow leaves on the ground in fall. I would tell my students to put their arms around the trunks to see how many people it took to encircle the trees. My grandfather said the buildings of the Old Crescent looked old *then*.

I stretch my arms around the history of the School of Education. It is a wistful smile but still a smile to know I cannot put my arms around it all.

Frederic W. Lieber
Author

# INTRODUCTION

The origin of the School of Education dates from 1829 when Indiana College created a preparatory department during the presidency of Andrew Wylie. Preparation was designed to ready students for collegiate work, more out of parental concern than applied pedagogy, which came later. Indiana College had succeeded Indiana Seminary, established in 1820.

Seminary square campus about 1850 from a photogravure produced about 1890.

The College became Indiana University in 1838. None of these schools was a religious institution, but all were led by preacher presidents until 1885.

Indiana University created a course in didactics in 1851. A normal department and model school followed in 1852. The course, department, and model school were steps toward the institutionalization of education. The entire university, of course, was devoted to education, but these more localized developments spelled a discipline of teaching and learning with its own elements and methods. Since education was generic to the university, the distinct role of such a discipline would be defined and defended. Initially, its growth came as much from outside as inside the academy, but the value of public education has fluctuated in American society as well.

Scholars disagree on the origin of "normal," but it meant a teacher training school. The Normal Department of 1852 begot a Department of Pedagogy in 1886 that begot a Department of Education in 1904 that begot a School of Education in 1908. Trustees of Indiana University authorized the School of Education to award its own degree in 1923. Today, in 2023, we celebrate the 100th anniversary of a professional school of education with duties and powers comparable to schools of law and medicine and other professional schools in the university that grant their own degrees.

So began the place we know today—a state, national, and international school in a major research university, housed in a five-story building with two wings; awarding degrees in nine undergraduate, 28 master's, and 29 doctoral programs; and with four specialist, 21 certificate, and 17 licensure programs. The school has come a long way from a course in didactics or a small house on Third Street in Bloomington, granting one degree to one student in 1925.

Alpha Hall, located on 3rd Street, served as the home of the IU School of Education in 1925.

Henry Lester Smith, fourth and longest serving dean, led the school from 1916 to 1946. Smith and his successor, Wendell W. Wright, dean until 1959, laid the professional foundation. Smith was the lever of growth. A graduate of IU, he was superintendent of Bloomington schools, received his doctorate from Columbia University, and came back to southern Indiana with fresh ideas of teacher education. During his tenure, the school established a graduate division, a school counselor curriculum, the Bureau of Cooperative Research, the University School, Bloomington conferences and headquarters of high school principals and superintendents, and courses for library science, physical education, home economics, nursing, and an administrator's license. Smith often locked horns with Fernandus Payne, dean of the University Graduate School, over the quality of the School of Education's graduate programs.

Wendell Wright during his tenure as dean, appointed scholars and good administrators. One of them, Raleigh Holmstedt, became president of Indiana State University. Wright expanded the guidance curriculum and created a global teacher development program. His international focus was higher education partnerships, whereas Smith had concentrated on secondary and elementary international projects. The school expanded cooperative doctoral programs and launched closed-circuit television broadcasts across campus and airborne television instruction throughout the state. A longtime advisor of IU President Herman B Wells, Wright was coauthor of the consequential campus self-study that Wells commissioned in 1937.

The school prospered so well under Smith and Wright that it was prepared to take advantage of vast federal expenditures in the post-World War II period. The GI Bill, National Defense Education Act of 1958, and Great Society programs of Lyndon Johnson flooded schools with money for scholarships, faculty, facilities, and research. In the 1960s the school was the largest of its kind in the nation, ranking second, with over 200 full-time faculty and millions of dollars in grants. David L. Clark, dean from 1966 to 1974, had worked as a federal educational research and development officer. A scholar of educational leadership, he preached the mantra of development and knew how to write grants. His term was a golden era for the school.

After Clark, the deluge. In the mid-1970s the federal goose had stopped laying golden eggs, the economy was in a downturn, enrollments were low, income was down, and University School faculty now had tenure in the School of Education. Sixty faculty lines were cut. Still, the school embraced the 1980s with an award-winning teacher education research project that lasted 20 years, innovations in instructional technology, nationally recognized research in group counseling, robust international engagements, a state coalition of teacher education programs, and a vibrant summer school. A decade begun in retrenchment ended on a high note. Howard Mehlinger, dean of the school from 1981 to 1990, won broad support for a multimillion-dollar education building on Seventh Street with state-of-the-art technology, now the school's home.

In 1990 University Dean Donald Warren took office, bearing a title that for the first time reflected the Bloomington dean's authority over education schools in Indianapolis and Bloomington. He served until 2000. Retirements during his tenure allowed him to reshape the school. He hired half the faculty. The next 10 years saw multidisciplinary teacher education reform; an award-winning student teaching office with global, urban, and Native American placements; approval for a counseling psychology program; advances in educational technology; an innovative survey of higher education; additions to the faculty of women and people of color; alignment of faculty salaries with Big Ten norms; expansion of the school's endowment; undergraduate, graduate student, and staff participation in school activities; and global partnerships in the Americas, China, Vietnam, and sub-Saharan Africa.

A cold bath awaited. The new millennium began with national attacks on underachieving schools because of the brightly named but poorly conceived federal policy, No Child Left Behind. In 2005, under the guise of accountability and reform, the state of Indiana began taking away from public education with one hand what it gave to vouchers and charter schools with the other. Not surprisingly, School of Education enrollments plummeted.

With unshakeable commitment to the greater good, however, coupled with strong advocacy and research innovations, the school advanced under its new leader, Gerardo Gonzalez, who took office in 2000. Second-longest-serving dean, Gonzalez was a fearless ambassador of the school and public education. His own history as a Cuban refugee gave him a genetic belief in the ladder of opportunity that is American education. He climbed and extended that ladder to all.

Speaking truth to power in the legislature and newspaper, Gonzalez unmasked the so-called reforms of the Indiana state superintendent of public instruction as not-so-veiled attempts to decertify teacher preparation and dismantle public education. Meanwhile in the school, the daily work of studying, teaching, research, and service moved forward.

A new strategic plan under Gonzalez strengthened school initiatives—teacher education, partnerships with public schools, research and creative activities, graduate programs, appropriate use of technology, international activities, and diversity. Faculty won awards for research on educational disadvantages of low-income children and therapeutic benefits of interpersonal verbal feedback. An influential survey of higher education quality based on student engagement began to gather data that would produce a reputation of national significance. The Indiana Center for Evaluation and the Indiana Education Policy Centers that had provided valuable research to the legislature became the Center for Evaluation and Education Policy, at work today. The first occupant accepted the Barbara B. Jacobs Chair of Education and Technology. A courageous effort to improve higher education for women and men in Afghanistan began, and a 20-year project of the Department of Counseling and Educational Psychology was well underway serving HIV-AIDS patients and healthcare workers in Botswana.

From 2015 to the present, the school has had three deans—Terrence Mason, Lemuel Watson, and Anastasia Morrone—but the worldwide news has been COVID-19. During the pandemic, the school continued to produce research and graduates in teaching, counseling, and leadership. The one-school, two-campus arrangement between Indianapolis and Bloomington dissolved. International partnerships and new degree programs began. Student teachers worked globally, and undergraduates enjoyed a new living-learning residence hall. Physical improvements brightened the education library, Center for Human Growth, and teacher education offices. Spanning these developments was the pain but also the nobility found in COVID-19. In an unprecedented move, the university closed, classes met online, and technology took center stage. The school emerged with renewed appreciation of its valiant community.

The school stands on the shoulders of giants who did not wait for the future to be handed to them—dedicated faculty, staff, and students who seized the moment for education, often against great odds. Today is a challenging time for public education, but the school continues to discover new meaning in its century-old tradition. If the past is any indication, the school will build on its strong foundation and find new ways, barely imaginable today, to inspire what the great 19th-century school reformer Caleb Mills called "a disciplined mind and cultivated heart."[1]

Caleb Mills.

# Timeline: 1787–1922

1787    "Education shall be forever encouraged": Ordinance of 1787 (Northwest Ordinance)

1816    Indiana Constitution provides for public education "wherein tuition shall be gratis, and equally open to all"

1820    Indiana Seminary established

1828    Indiana Seminary is Indiana College

1829    Preparatory Department created

1838    Indiana College is Indiana University

1851    First class in didactics

1852    IU trustees authorize Normal Department and model school

1886    Normal Department is Department of Pedagogy

1891    Education is an academic major

1895    First course in psychology and pedagogy

1901    IU's first international project led by education professor Elmer Burritt Bryan in the Philippines

1902    William Lowe Bryan is 10th president of Indiana University, serves 35 years

1904    Department of Pedagogy is Department of Education, begins systematic supervision of teaching

1908    Department of Education is School of Education; President Bryan is acting dean for three years

1914    Bureau of Cooperative Research; Bureau of Visual Education has 14 lantern slide sets

1916    Henry Lester Smith is third dean and serves 30 years

1922    High School Principals' Conference begins in Bloomington

# CHAPTER 1

# Answering a Call, Becoming a School (1820–1922)

Institutions as well as individuals respond to a call. When success is not immediate and rewards are distant, it takes more than worldly income to stay the course for hard-won outcomes. It takes a calling—something like the moral equivalent of love, renewed by understanding, to listen to human need and respond with dedication. Today's teachers, counselors, and educational leaders are pioneers of promise descended from women and men who believed in Indiana University and its School of Education.

Always a refuge in times of adversity, education has had adversity of its own. The success of Indiana University and its School of Education was hard-won. For many years there was no money from the state. Enrollments were low. Fires destroyed buildings. Many Hoosiers doubted public support for schools. The achievements of the university and school testify to people who kept faith in education. Despite hostility and ambivalence, they achieved magnificence. How the 19th and early 20th centuries issued a call that people answered for the greater good is the story of this chapter.

The rhetoric of education, if not the reality, described the state of Indiana and Indiana University before either came into existence. The state and its namesake university share an ancestor in the Northwest Ordinance of 1787. The Ordinance enabled Indiana to become a state. At the same time, it advocated the spread of education in the states that it created. Article Three of the Ordinance reads: "Religion, Morality, and knowledge being necessary to good government and the happiness of mankind, Schools and the means of education shall forever be encouraged."[2] The Ordinance was the first attempt of the United States Congress to acknowledge the value of education in lands that became Indiana, Ohio, Illinois, Michigan, Wisconsin, and Minnesota.

Acknowledgment, however, is all that happened. The first Indiana Constitution of 1816 incorporated Congress's offer to set aside the 16th section of each township in new states for school purposes, but the offer did not provide much money because land was plentiful and cheap. The Indiana Seminary in Bloomington was approved in 1820 and opened in 1825 with 10 students and one teacher. Its name was changed to Indiana College in 1828 and it became Indiana University in 1838. For its first 47 years, Indiana University and its predecessors received no funds from the state. The University survived on interest from the sale of lands, rents on unsold land, and tuition.[3] It had 11 acres of land and three buildings in 1820.[4]

The challenges of Indiana University in the 19th century highlight the struggle of education and the prehistory of the school. Confronting the university until after the Civil War was uneven leadership, low enrollment, debate over a classical versus practical curriculum, difficulty finding qualified faculty, charges of elitism, weak finances, construction costs, fires, sectarian squabbles, public disinterest in education, opposition to tax-supported schools, and inequities of gender, race, and economic class. These challenges also reflected the state's new mix of urban and rural populations, and business and farming interests.

The question of tax-supported education was especially divisive. In winter 1846–1847, in response to an amendment to levy a tax for school purposes, fierce opposition ignited in the state legislature. "Fireworks" were recounted in a report to the Board of Trustees of the Public Schools of Indianapolis. The controversy was a cold political baptism of Indiana University, not yet 10 years old:

> The amendment [to raise a tax for schools] met with vigorous and determined opposition from several influential members. The new notion, imported, it was feared, from the Atlantic seaboard, that the property of the community should educate its children, was denounced as an experiment and a heresy, unjust, inequitable, and worthy of its Puritan origin. The inexpediency of any taxation, except for roads and the support of government, including the General Assembly, was resolutely urged in opposition. Certain rough, and, in a robust way, popular members from the unterrified districts, were earnest in condemning common schools on general principles. They and their fathers never had an education, and they had achieved Legislative honors without such aid; likewise their children might attain the same dignity, if not spoiled by learning. Schooling led to extravagance and folly, law and ruin. A man could keep store, chop wood, physic, plow, plead and preach without an education, and what more was needed? The fleetest, long-nosed, deep-rooting hogs, and most flexible hoop-poles spring spontaneously from the soil. Without the aid of Science, Nature had enriched us with the fruitfulest powers of mud. The wilderness of Indiana had been subdued, and teeming crops grew luxuriant over the graves of dead savages—all done by unlearned men.[5]

Despite the charge that education led to law and ruin, positive signs were visible on the horizon, especially for the professionalization of education. In language at least, the state law creating the Indiana Seminary in 1820 endorsed democratic principles of equity and equality. It urged a public school system "ascending the regular gradation from Township Schools to a state seminary, wherein tuition shall be gratis and equally open to all," with no distinctions made between rich and poor.[6] Andrew Wylie, the university's first president, created a preparatory department in 1829 (a proto-high school) to elevate prospective university students. Latin and Greek were the fare of the curriculum.

In 1852 the legislature designated Indiana University as the "University of the State," heading the state's educational system. That same year was when the legislature ordered Indiana University to establish a normal school. The board of trustees of the university eagerly responded by authorizing a normal department and school, saying, "There is no measure in regard to the State University more urgently required by public opinion than this. Through this department the common school system of the state will be brought into connexion and sympathy with the University."[7] It had been 36 years since the Indiana constitution called for free public education, a goal achieved when reformers awakened the conscience of the legislature. No reformer was more responsible for that awakening than Caleb Mills.

Mills came to Indiana in 1833 from Dartmouth College and Andover Theological Seminary when he was 27 years old. He was the first professor at Wabash College and the second state superintendent of schools in Indiana. He wrote a series of six letters addressed to the Indiana legislature from 1846 to 1852, and to the Constitutional Convention of 1852, signed "One of the People." Mills' letters caused one Indiana historian to say of them, "They are without doubt the most important document ever prepared on the subject of education in Indiana."[8] Mills advocated raising tax revenues for public schools; securing competent teachers by means of training, supervision, and higher salaries; providing suitable textbooks; arousing public concern for education; and raising standards of admission, graduation, and professional degrees in institutions of higher learning.[9]

Engraved in limestone on the old education building in Bloomington at Third and Jordan (now Eagleson) where the school moved in 1938–1939 is an inscription from Mills: "Teachers must inspire as well as instruct."

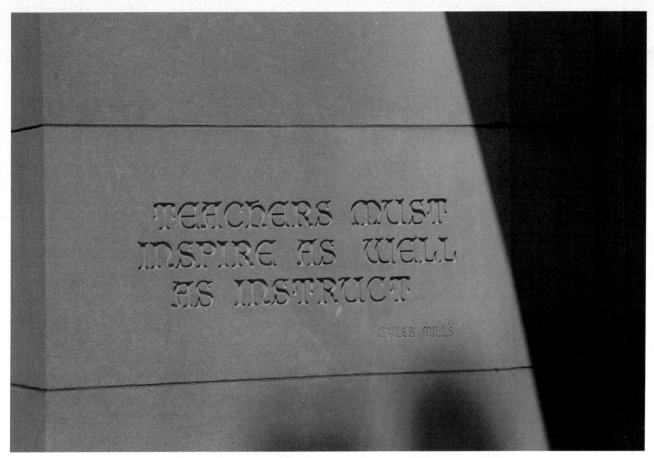

Inscription at the entryway to the current School of Education building.
This was also inscribed on the previous building.

The title of this book, *A Disciplined Mind and Cultivated Heart*, comes from a quote of his inscribed above the stage in Caleb Mills Auditorium at Shortridge High School, opened in 1864 as Indianapolis High School.

Indiana University had already anticipated the recommendations that Mills advocated. The university created a professorship in 1839 to prepare teachers for the common schools. President Wylie had tried to get funds for a normal school from 1838 through 1850. Finally, in 1851 the board of trustees authorized the university to organize a class in didactics with a view to establishing a normal department. A report of the board of trustees to the Indiana General Assembly in 1852 proposed a model school that would

> present to the eye of the learner, a common school, as nearly perfect as possible in its order, arrangement, furniture, classification, and methods of teaching. This school [will serve] also as a school of practice, in which to exercise and test the young teacher's ability and tact.[10]

The legislature provided no funds for a model school, but the university pressed ahead and opened it. Fire caused the model school to close in 1854. Despite its short-lived tenure, the school was a prescient idea, anticipating by almost 80 years the School of Education's laboratory school, authorized in 1937, known as the University School or U-School.

Students at the University School in 1957.

Students outside School of Education in front of inscription, "Teachers must inspire as well as instruct" in 1951.

In 1852–1853 Professor Daniel Reed's didactics course enrolled 22 men and 12 women, and it was a popular summer offering. The opening of the Indiana State Normal School in Terre Haute (now Indiana State University) in 1870 caused a hiatus in teacher training, however, as it became the premier normal school in the state. The Preparatory Department closed in 1873, also in response to a preparatory school opened in 1873 that became Bloomington High School in 1885.[11] Much later, preparing students was reprised as the Junior College under IU President Herman B Wells to gear up World War II veterans for campus life. More recently, with an emphasis on advising, the Junior College morphed into the University Division, and because of academic enrichments in secondary schools, the education and business schools became the first to benefit from direct admission of students from high school. High-achieving students can now enroll immediately in their respective schools upon admission to the university, bypassing the University Division and prerequisite courses.

In 1885 David Starr Jordan assumed office as seventh president of Indiana University and was a reliable supporter of teacher training. Jordan was the first scientist, nonclergy president. He created the elective curriculum, which became popular among students. In 1886 the university established the Department of Pedagogy, headed by its sole faculty member Richard G. Boone, professor of pedagogics. The department took a leading role in summer sessions, foreshadowing the extraordinary growth that the School of Education would bring to summer school, extension courses, and continuing and adult education, to the benefit of the university.

Anticipating the popularity of educational psychology, the school started a course in psychology and pedagogy in 1895. The alliance of psychology and teaching was a productive integration in the 20th and 21st centuries, as well, contributing to the growth of graduate and undergraduate programs and departments in the school and integrating counseling and psychology in teacher education.

Psychologist by training and professor of philosophy, William Lowe Bryan became the 10th president of Indiana University in 1902. He had already taught a course on teaching in 1885 in the Philosophy Department and had published important psychological research on learning. Prominent member of the second generation of American psychologists and the student of G. Stanley Hall, Bryan was a contemporary of William James, dean of American psychology.

Bryan recognized the intersection of art and science in teaching, shared by his colleague John A. Bergstrom, professor of psychology and pedagogy. In 1897 Bergstrom proposed using the state as a laboratory for the direct study of schoolwork and its problems in cities and towns. With Bryan's support, Bergstrom organized site visits by students and instructors and arranged practice teaching and training of superintendents across the state.

William Lowe Bryan.

The end of the 19th century and the first two decades of the 20th century secured the discipline of education as science, practice, and profession in the university. The rise of science, the delineation of disciplines, and the large number of high schools contributed to an increase in postsecondary enrollments and fueled careers in teaching. In 1897 Indiana passed a compulsory education law that greatly expanded attendance in schools and enrollment in the university.

Teacher supervision became more systematic, critic teachers were employed in city high schools, and the IU Department of Pedagogy became the Department of Education. The renamed department made good use of Bloomington schools for teacher training in the field. In 1907 the legislature organized teachers into classifications. A minimum wage was established by the Indiana State Board of Education, and Indiana University was accredited to train teachers of all grade levels.

The IU Department of Education became the School of Education in 1908, with President Bryan as acting dean. He served three years. It was the third time he had assumed a position of leadership in teacher training. From 1908 to 1909 the School of Education had 605 students, but enrollment and degrees were handled in the College of Arts and Sciences.[12] Henry Lester Smith became dean of the school in 1916. He had been superintendent of schools in Bloomington in 1909 and director of school supervision and administrative practice in the School of Education. Before becoming dean, Smith directed IU summer sessions. He was in the vanguard of public school teachers as civic leaders.

Henry Lester Smith.

The first woman to be granted an honorary degree by Indiana University was an Indianapolis teacher and administrator of elementary education named Nebraska Cropsey, nominated in 1913 by another teacher, Robert I. Hamilton, university trustee and former superintendent of the Madison County schools. An auditorium in the Indianapolis-Marion County Public Library is named after Cropsey. Also in Indianapolis, vocational education began in the Extension Center in 1918.

The stage was set for the School of Education as a degree-granting unit of the university. The school's ability to grant its own degree took pressure off the College of Arts and Sciences for enrollment, class assignment, and other bureaucratic functions. An education degree paved the way to the professionalization of teaching, counseling, and educational leadership. The Normal Department was distant history, and current events held promise. University expansion following World War I was extensive. Enrollment and faculty salaries were up, and celebration was in the air. Special trains brought crowds to Bloomington for the university's centennial in January 1920.[13] The School of Education was poised for growth. The future was in its hands as never before.

# Timeline: 1923–2023

1923    School of Education authorized to award its own degree

1924    *Bulletin of the School of Education* publishes for 45 years, continues as *Viewpoints* (1970–1977)

1929    Graduate Division

1932    First doctor of education degree

1937    University School dedicated, opens in 1938 in a building funded by the Works Progress Administration without room for classes or offices

1946    Wendell W. Wright is dean

        Units of the school: elementary, secondary, nursing, library science, vocational, and distributive education; division of research and field services, Institute of Educational Research, and graduate division

1951    New wing added to the University School at Third and Jordan (now Eagleson)

        First issue of *Chalkboard*

        School of Education Alumni Association

1954    Thailand contract

1959    Harold G. Shane is dean

        Midwest Program for Airborne Television Instruction

1960    Institute for Child Study; Boyd McCandless, director

1964    University School moves to 10th and the Bypass; school takes over vacated space at Third and Jordan (now Eagleson)

1965    Philip Peak is acting dean

        The school has 10 divisions: administration, adult education, educational media, foundations of human behavior, higher education, instruction and curriculum, international contracts, library science, research, and University School

1966    David L. Clark is dean

1967    Human Relations Committee established to respond to student unrest (James Walden and James Weigand, coexecutive secretaries)

1969    Dean Cark invites students to "sit in" and air grievances

        Center for Innovation in Teaching the Handicapped

        Bureau of Educational Studies and Testing (BEST)

1970    Monroe County Community School Corporation takes over the University School

        Center for Human Growth

1972    Division of Teacher Education, funded by US Department of Health, Education, and Welfare: Leo Fay, director

        *Bulletin of the School of Education* is *Viewpoints*

1974    Richard P. Gousha is dean

        Schools of education in Bloomington and Indianapolis merge

| 1975 | The school has five divisions: administration and administrative studies; foundations of human behavior, instruction and curriculum, teacher education, and instructional systems technology |
|---|---|

1975   The school has five divisions: administration and administrative studies; foundations of human behavior, instruction and curriculum, teacher education, and instructional systems technology

Smith Research Center opens in former University School at 10th and the Bypass

Education Building is Wendell W. Wright School of Education Building

1976   Maris M. Proffitt and Mary Higgins Proffitt bequest

Mathematics Education Development Center

1978   Divisions become departments: administration and administrative studies; art education; counseling and guidance; curriculum and instruction; educational psychology; history, philosophy, and comparative studies in education; instructional systems technology; language education; mathematics, science, and social studies; special education; vocational education, business education, distributive education, and home economics

First Proffitt Award for outstanding dissertation

1980   Laurence D. Brown is acting dean

1981   Howard Mehlinger is dean

1982   Indiana University-Purdue University Indianapolis School of Education dedicated

1983   Howard Mehlinger creates Board of Visitors

1984   Coalition of Teacher Education Programs

1990   Donald Warren is dean

1992   New W. W. Wright Education Building opens, the school's current home

1994   Dean's Advisory Council

1996   Armstrong Teacher Educator Award

1997   School-wide reform of teacher education

1998   Barbara B. Jacobs Chair in Education and Technology

1999   National Survey of Student Engagement

Center for Research on Learning and Technology

2000   Gerardo Gonzalez is dean

2002   Long-Range Strategic Plan

2004   Center for Evaluation and Education Policy

2011   IU's first online doctoral degree, EdD in instructional systems technology

2014   The school's first living-learning undergraduate center, INSPIRE

2015   Terrence Mason is interim dean and dean the following year

2016   Elder Watson Diggs "The Dreamer" Award in honor of the first African American to graduate from the school (in 1916)

2017   IU Board of Trustees approves separation of Bloomington and Indianapolis campuses

2018   Lemuel Watson is dean

2020   University moves to online in spring due to COVID-19 outbreak, is hybrid for the next year

Anastasia Morrone is interim dean, and dean in 2021

Global Gateway for Teachers is 50 years old

2023   School of Education celebrates its 100th birthday as a degree-granting unit of the university

# CHAPTER 2

# A Strong Professional Foundation (1923–1957)

Prior to his presidential inauguration in 1902, William Lowe Bryan considered Indiana University "for the most part a large teacher's college."[14] Although he created the School of Education, Bryan had broader plans for the university. He looked beyond teacher preparation, as important as it was. Population, industry, commerce, and cities were growing rapidly. He was determined that the university respond to the needs of a fast-expanding state. Bryan's strategy was to create professional schools around a core of liberal arts studies. Development of such schools was his most significant achievement, although he himself thought making 29 budgets was his chief accomplishment.[15]

Bryan was a modernist in classicist clothing. A pioneering researcher in the new discipline of experimental psychology, he taught philosophy, pedagogy, Latin, and Greek. He was a humanist by heart with a scientific mind. It is appropriate that a multidisciplinary scholar started the multidisciplinary School of Education.

Bryan was the immediate cause, but the professionalization of education was an accumulation of factors—proliferation of high schools, increased undergraduate enrollment, demand for university-educated teachers, urbanization, industrialization, and a psychology-based pedagogy. The legislative impetus was a study by the Indiana Educational Commission (the Bachman Survey), commissioned by the legislature in the early 1920s, that was critical of the control that the IU College of Arts and Sciences had over the School of Education. The study recommended "a genuine School of Education."[16]

IU had canceled its Preparatory Department in 1873. By then, high schools were sending qualified applicants to the university. Extension and summer school programs were novel and popular. In 1900 the School of Education began to establish educational standards and practices for the state. The school was active beyond Indiana as well. In 1901 IU alumnus and education professor Elmer Burritt Bryan became principal of the Insular Normal School in the Philippines. Two years later he was Superintendent of Education. He employed 800 American teachers, many of them IU graduates, and encouraged Filipino students to further their education at IU.[17]

The school's international work prompted IU Vice President for International Affairs Patrick O'Meara to recognize the school's influence: "Early in the twentieth century, Indiana University faculty members in education started the university's long and substantial history of assisting with overseas projects."[18]

Expansion of the school and university was well underway at the turn of the century. The school established a Teachers Agency in 1904 to help graduates find jobs. The Indiana accrediting law of 1907 required 12 weeks' training for prospective teachers. The number of IU graduates becoming teachers was increasing.

Already, between 1871 and 1880, the proportion of teacher-graduates was up 14%. From 1895 to 1900, it was up 61%.[19] In the 1900–1901 academic year, the university had 1,137 full-time students; in the 1929–1930 academic year, 5,762.[20] 1920 was the first time the total budget of the university exceeded $1 million.[21]

President Bryan acknowledged the obvious in 1922 when he told the board of trustees, I recommend the reorganization of the School of Education on a basis comparable to the basis on which the other schools of the University are organized and granting to the School of Education the duties and powers that are ordinarily granted to similar schools in other state institutions.[22]

Bryan served three years as acting dean of the new school. As a psychologist, he knew the importance of learning. He advocated exposure to advanced models to train teachers. If Bryan professionalized the school, its indispensable early deans were Henry Lester Smith and Wendell W. Wright. They served consecutively for a total of 43 years. In 1916 Bryan, the university's longest serving president, appointed Smith, the School of Education's longest serving dean. Smith led the school for 30 years through two world wars. Smith was the lever of growth; Wright, dean from 1946 to 1959, consolidated the gains. These deans laid the professional foundation for the School of Education.

Incoming dean of the School of Education meets the outgoing dean.

Born in Bloomington, Henry Lester Smith lived most of his 87 years in the Monroe County area. He graduated from IU in 1898 and received his doctorate in 1916 from Teachers College, Columbia University. Smith's grandparents were abolitionists. He wrote about the Underground Railroad in Monroe County.[23] Promotion of the School of Education was paramount in his 1916 letter to President Bryan, after becoming dean: "My confidence in the ultimate outcome of this venture is based upon your policy of putting the School of Education on the highest possible plane."[24]

In 1922 the School of Education included five full-time faculty; 11 critic teachers; four staff; programs in vocational, elementary, and secondary education, and school administration; and a Bureau of Coöperative Research. The Bureau conducted studies on school finance, teacher supply and demand, techniques of handling large classes, and school administration, among other topics. Smith directed the bureau from 1916 until his retirement.

Smith worked closely with the Indiana Department of Public Instruction and the Indiana State Teachers Association. He was president of the National Education Association from 1934 to 1935, and secretary-general of the World Federation of Education Associations from 1941 to 1946.

The end of World War I brought an influx of students and changes to campus. In 1918 vocational education began at the Extension Center in Indianapolis. A year later, Smith directed IU's burgeoning summer sessions and served in that capacity until his retirement. Teachers constituted one third of summer enrollments.

In 1924 the Bureau of Cooperative Research launched the *Bulletin of the School of Education*, continued as *Viewpoints* from 1970 to 1977. The *Bulletin* had a national audience and authorship and featured a wide range of educational research. Besides the *Bulletin*, the bureau published a bibliography of educational tests and measures and sponsored annual conferences for psychometricians, high school principals, and elementary school supervisors. The conferences and the *Bulletin* were the oldest of their kind in the United States.

The 1920s and 1930s saw innovations in continuing and adult education, school psychology, a graduate division, commercial development of audio-visual (A-V) aids, and nursing and library courses. The era's racial politics required innovative thinking. In 1934 Smith arranged for the school to pay train travel to Indianapolis for several Black students to do their student teaching. Black students could only teach in "a colored high school," and Bloomington lacked one at the time.[25]

Cover of the 1927 issue of *the Bulletin of the School of Education Indiana University*. Inscription at top reads, "Presented to Indiana University Library by Henry Lester Smith."

Nathaniel Sayles                Ernest Stevenson                Evelyn White

George Wade                    George Porter

Students required to travel from Bloomington to Indianapolis to complete their required
student teaching at the then segregated Crispus Attucks High School.

By 1937 the School of Education was training teachers and special workers in rural and urban settings, and at primary, intermediate, and secondary levels. Beyond the core curriculum, the school taught commercial subjects, home economics, music, art, physical education, health, library work, and special needs, in graded and ungraded schools. In 1929 the school offered its first master's degree, and in 1932, its first EdD degree.

The School of Education was the largest professional school in the university in the 1930s, enrolling more than 20% of students studying in Bloomington. More than 30% of graduate degrees in the university were awarded to education majors.[26] The School of Health, Physical Education, and Recreation spun off from the School of Education during that period, as did nursing and library science.

Herman B Wells became president of Indiana University in 1937. One of his first acts was to create the Self Survey Committee to examine all aspects of the university and report recommendations. Faculty acceptance of the study's frank recommendations, chief among which was improvement of university teaching, was a blueprint for growth. Wendell W. Wright, professor of education and later dean of the School of Education, was one of three faculty-authors of the study. Wells's reliance on Wright throughout his presidency proved beneficial to the school. Wells championed the school and was a passionate promoter of international programs, an area in which the school was a pioneering leader.

Herman B Wells.

In 1938 the School of Education Laboratory School (University School) opened at Third and Jordan (now Eagleson) in a building proposed by the Olmsted Brothers company and funded by the Works Progress Administration. University School was a cooperative project of the Monroe County school system and the School of Education. At its inception, it enrolled over 600 schoolchildren from kindergarten through high school. The school was an incubator and demonstration site for new ideas in teacher training and instructional technology.

Jens Zorn, now a retired professor of physics at the University of Michigan, was a graduate of the University School. He entered it as a sophomore in 1946 when his father joined the IU Department of Mathematics. Reflecting on his experience much later, he said, "I came from a large urban high school and graduated in Bloomington in a class of not 100. Instead of an anonymous face, I had to be engaged, or there would be no teams or school plays. It was warm and friendly and transformational, and the education could hardly have been better. Teachers knew us and took care of us. It was not a high-pressure place, but we had decent challenges for our abilities. There was an extraordinary number of student teachers. We had a sort of sport in flummoxing them in mathematics."[27]

Some things have not changed.

While the School of Education's international leadership expanded under Wells, an equally compelling strength was the development of A-V materials, first located in the Extension Division. Over time, the development of A-V materials became its own department under various names, including, eventually, the Department of Instructional Systems Technology (IST). The founder of IST was Lawrence C. Larson, a science teacher and high school principal in Iowa, experienced in industry and adult education. Larson came to IU in 1940, the only faculty member in A-V education in the school. He had a joint appointment in the Extension Division in Adult Education and Public Services.

Lantern slide projector from the 1950s.

Starting out with a small collection of lantern slides and films in what was then known as the Bureau of Audio-Visual Aids, Larson showed "entrepreneurial behavior."[28] President Wells often traveled by train, and "surprisingly" Larson would show up sitting next to him. Wells could be counted on to find money when Larson needed it. Later, the President's train schedules were not made public.[29] Ever the entrepreneur, Larson used funds from film rental, sales, and public television distribution to hire academics who were scholars and practitioners, not from traditional media or technology backgrounds. He developed graduate programs in Africa, the Middle East, and Southeast Asia. Today, IST has alumni in 120 countries.

Carolyn Guss, Harvey Frye, and James Knowlton were among the pioneers that Larson attracted to the department. At the time of Larson's death in 1972, IST had grown from 1 to 28 faculty members. It had 200 doctoral graduates and contract services in Nigeria, Sierra Leone, Mali, Puerto Rico, the US Virgin Islands, and Brazil.

In 1942 IU faculty approved the Junior Division in response to the "nagging realization" and "haunting perception," since 1825, of large numbers of poorly prepared and unmotivated students. Those numbers were exacerbated by the onrush of World War II veterans.[30] New services were needed for intensive testing, counseling and guidance, and improvement of first-year courses. Wells appointed Wendell Wright dean of the Junior Division. Wright developed individual counseling services for beginning students.

Wright became dean of the School of Education in 1946 after serving as director of elementary education. Of the transition from Smith to Wright, Herman Wells wrote: "The School of Education was one of the most active in the international-technical assistance field. Dean Smith had been a pioneer leader in international education at the elementary and secondary levels. Dean Wright followed in his footsteps and broadened the base of interest to include the university level as well."[31]

Dean Wendell W. Wright at head of conference table in 1951. Table is now
located in the current School of Education building.

The university experienced tremendous expansion following the Second World War. The GI Bill, signed in 1944, sent two million students into the nation's colleges and universities. From 1945 to 1951, the increase in full-time School of Education faculty was 175%. The increase in total student enrollment in the school (undergraduate and graduate) for the same period was 254%. Besides university-wide growth, these percentages reflect the increasing complexity, popularity, and diversity of the school. Disciplines of nursing; library science; home economics; and health, physical education, and recreation were part of the school.

In 1947 School 42 in Indianapolis was named for Elder Watson Diggs, the first African American graduate of the School of Education, who received his BA in 1911 and later his MA in education. While at IU, Diggs founded what is now known as Kappa Alpha Psi national fraternity.

Elder Watson Diggs (center, above "DI" in INDIANA) at a house party
for Kappa Alpha Nu (later renamed Kappa Alpha Psi) in 1911.

Elder Watson Diggs.

A scholarship/fellowship was created in Diggs's name and is still being awarded.

Graduate programs were expanding. At the same time, the school faced pushback within the university. When the school wanted to offer a PhD degree through the Graduate School, opposition arose. The views of one faculty member in the College of Arts and Sciences illustrated the problem. Reflecting later on the problem, Lander MacClintock, professor of French and Italian, said:

> Those of us in the academic disciplines, many of us, felt that the School of Education was not the—that it really had no place in the University—that the training of teachers was the function of the teachers' colleges....Then, also, there was considerable difference as to the nature of the degree given by the School of Education. The College of Arts and Sciences thought that the doctor's degree [in education] should be definitely a professional degree, and they felt that the subject matter taught as graduate work in the School of Education wasn't sufficiently reliable—not sufficiently a discipline—to be introduced into a University.[32]

MacClintock's opinion at the time was shared by influential IU professors such as Fernandus Payne, dean of the Graduate School, and Stith Thompson in folklore who would become dean of the Graduate School. During a heated debate, Payne said: "The spirit and zeal of the educationists are those of the missionary who cannot be satisfied until every heathen is converted by persuasion or force to his way of thinking."[33] Heathens or not, Deans Smith and Wright were persuasive educationists, and the school eventually prevailed in the Graduate School; but the rhetoric across campus demonstrated visceral criticism of the school.

In 1948 the school embarked on a cooperative program that allowed students to pursue the Doctor of Education degree at participating campuses. The first members were IU, Indiana State Teachers College, and Ball State Teachers College. Membership grew to include 14 cooperating institutions from Florida to Appalachia and from Nebraska to the Carolinas.

Old and new generations of leadership reunited in 1951 when Henry Lester Smith and Wendell W. Wright opened the School of Education building in a new wing built onto the University School.

Construction of new wing being added to the University School in 1950.

In his remarks Smith said: "Migratory movements of the School of Education headquarters have reached a coveted and long-awaited resting point...from Science Hall to the old Theta House to Mottier House to Alpha Hall, and at last to the newly constructed wing at the south end of the University School." Wright said, "Approximately one-fifth of students who attend this University are interested in teaching as a profession. We shape our buildings and they in turn shape us." President Wells added, "In the last 113 years, Indiana University has made many contributions to the welfare of the State, but in no field has the University's work been finer than in teacher education."[34]

Growth began to diversify. The School of Education Alumni Association held its inaugural banquet in the early 1950s. The University School was no longer able to provide on-site student teaching for all candidates, so a professional semester became necessary to furnish practice teaching throughout the state. With a fivefold increase in campus enrollment in the postwar period, the ratio of students to professor in the School of Education introduced a new impersonality into graduate and undergraduate programs.

As a result of these and other changes, the Committee on Teacher Education placed a new focus on teacher competency that included "disposition for further self-growth, ability to participate in democratic ways in group situation, capacity to respond to individuals as persons," a fifth year in teacher education, and improvements in licensing, extension programs, and professional standards.[35]

In fall 1953 a new course, Internship Training in Guidance, helped meet the need for supervised school guidance. The course was open to full-time graduate students who were placed in schools in Bloomington and surrounding areas. Cold War funding from federal agencies soon underwrote a major expansion in counselor education.

From 1953 to 1954, educational philosopher Stafford Clayton conducted a study of school governance, calling for a coordinating council with five committees, the ancestor of the school's current Policy Council. Such reforms in teacher education and school organization were part of a long-standing tradition of adapting teaching, counseling, and leadership to new social realities. Institutionalization of change became a signature effort of self-critical education.

In 1954 the school began a major, eight-year project to support teacher education in Thailand.

Dean Wright in Thailand with students from Thammasat University in 1955.

Dean Wright went to Thailand to develop a bachelor's degree program. Over the life of the project, senior IU faculty helped Thailand build a public education infrastructure that included a new graduate program in the Department of Education at Chulalongkorn University.

Art education received a boost in the late-1950s. Multicultural art, studio art for elementary and secondary students, and art appreciation were part of the postwar cultural zeitgeist. Frederick V. Mills received his EdD in elementary education and later joined the faculty. Along with Guy Hubbard and Mary Jane Rouse, both of whom came to the faculty from Stanford University in the early 1960s, he built art education in the school with textbooks for elementary teachers and a structured art education program. Hubbard pioneered the use of digital technologies and computer-generated images in art education curricula.

By the end of the first half of the 20th century, in the aftermaths of two world wars and during the deanships of Smith and Wright and the presidencies of Bryan and Wells, the School of Education had forged a strong professional foundation with national and international influence. In 1957 the school looked very different from its 1923 self, boasting a new building; a thriving laboratory school integrated with teacher education; record numbers of students, faculty, and staff; new instructional materials; extensive international engagements; systematic guidance of graduate and undergraduate students; reforms of teacher education; far-reaching research; rapid growth in services to the state; coordination with other divisions of the university; and a profusion of extension and adult education services. It is hard to imagine more expansion was on the way.

Acceleration of postwar growth and the influx of federal funding from the National Defense Education Act of 1958 and Lyndon Johnson's Great Society greeted a new generation of leaders in the school. Harold G. Shane was dean from 1959 to 1965; and Philip Peak was acting dean from 1965 to 1966. Their administrations witnessed developments in programmed teaching; educational radio broadcasts; partnerships in Pakistan, Sierra Leone, Saudi Arabia, Uruguay, and Thailand; a new institute of child study; an English curriculum study center; and the coordination of all university adult education services in the school.

(L to R) Harold G. Shane, Henry Lester Smith, and Wendell W. Wright.

It was David L. Clark, however, dean in 1966, who ushered in the era of unprecedented growth in the school. Clark brought with him into the deanship a seasoned hand in research and development and a keen understanding of grant writing, both at the federal level. His bold vision and research acumen paved the way for a blockbuster epoch in the school's history.

David L. Clark.

# CHAPTER 3

# The Golden Era (1958–1973)

The School of Education approached its sixth decade in solid shape—it was a full, professional partner in the university, well respected at home and abroad. Its academic programs were thriving; its services, essential to the state. Enrollments were strong. A new wing on an old building consolidated offices and activities. Faculty and staff were productive. Graduates held positions of prominence throughout the world. One area ripe for development was research.

Research is the lingua franca of prestige in institutions of higher learning. Before the Second World War when liberal arts faculty at IU argued that the School of Education had no place in the university, it was the research of its faculty and the quality of its graduate programs that earned equal citizenship. After the war, no credentials of the school were more important for academic standing than research. No sign of that standing was more evident than research centers and institutes. According to the IU Archives, from 1958 to 1973, the School of Education operated 29 research centers and institutes in the following areas: evaluation, social studies, teaching the handicapped, mathematics development, professional development, field services, child study, association of colleges and schools, elementary school principals, Indiana school boards, career guidance, pupil personnel programs for urban schools, Latino affairs, development of training materials, reading practicum, public choice in education, coalition of teacher education programs, innovations in teacher education, campus-community counseling, Libyan education, English language teaching, administrative studies, urban and multicultural education, innovations in human resource development, options for public education, experiential education, educational change, laboratory for educational development, and programmed teaching, research, and development.[36]

Much of the federal money came from the National Defense Education Act of 1958 (NDEA); post-Sputnik legislation; the Department of Health, Education, and Welfare (HEW); the Elementary and Secondary Education Act of 1965, a centerpiece of Lyndon Johnson's War on Poverty; the National Science Foundation; and the National Institutes of Health. Private funding sources included the Rockefeller, Ford, and Russell Sage foundations. The NDEA was the first direct federal funding to higher education in the nation's history. The school expanded counseling and guidance programs, early scholar grants, and faculty ranks. Thanks to teacher deferments in the early years of the Vietnam War, 10% of university undergraduates were enrolled annually in a new introductory teacher education course conceived and taught by newly hired education professor, Tom Gregory. Baby boomers filled university classrooms in numbers not seen since their parents came to campus on the GI Bill. The School of Education from the middle 1960s to the middle 1970s was "the largest producer of initially certified teachers in the country."[37]

Space limitations of the present book prevent a full accounting of each center and institute. The story of one center might serve as an example. In 1965 a 33-year-old social psychologist named Samuel Guskin joined the special education faculty. Having received his PhD from the University of North Carolina, he was working as a research associate professor of psychology at George Peabody College for Teachers under Nicholas Hobbs, chairman of the division of human development. At Peabody, Guskin met Howard Spicker in special education, who later joined the School of Education in Bloomington.

David L. Clark became dean of the School of Education in 1966. Clark had been director of the Cooperative Research Program, US Office of Education, a division of HEW, before becoming associate dean and professor of education at Ohio State University. His experience with federal grants was invaluable to coprincipal investigators Guskin and Spicker and their "brilliant grad student," Nettie R. Bartell, when they applied for and received funding to create a center for special education in 1969.[38]

William W. Lynch, professor and chairman of the IU Department of Educational Psychology, offered crucial administrative assistance. Earlier, on leave from the School of Education, Lynch had been a research fellow at Peabody, where he met Guskin. After a name change, the Center for Innovation in Teaching the Handicapped (CITH) was up and running with a five-year, $2.5-million allocation from HEW. The grant was the largest in the school up to that time.

Sam Guskin was the first director of the center. Melvyn Semmel, a graduate student of Guskin's at Peabody, succeeded him as director. The CITH was an interdisciplinary venture that brought together faculty in special education, child psychology, educational psychology, speech and hearing, and sociology. Robert B. Cairns, associate professor in the IU Department of Psychology, was a member of the research and development faculty of the center. Also on the affiliate faculty was Egon Guba, professor of education and director of the National Institute for the Study of Educational Change, an institute in the school. Converted from quantitative ranks, Guba became a nationally recognized theorist of qualitative methodology.

The CITH conducted basic research on labeling and stereotyping of people with disabilities, research methodology, and mainstreaming. It did work in development as well. Development for Clark meant "the search for generalizable solutions to operating problems in schools." He believed that besides adding to what is known about a field of study, a professional school of education should develop products "which can be deployed in carrying out social functions."[39] The center produced research on programmed tutoring. It published in-service training for teachers and student teachers based on observational studies of student–teacher and parent–teacher interactions with children with disabilities.

In 1952 the School of Education celebrated a century of teacher education. The school responded to social needs but now on a wider, more diverse scale. For instance, in the late 1950s the International Reading Association broke off from the National Council of Teachers of English (NCTE) because the NCTE did not want to teach reading. Consequently, education professor Leo Fay started a Department of Reading. It was a timely and productive effort. Illiteracy was a national crisis, highlighted by *Why Johnny Can't Read*, a 1955 exposé that showed graduates of high school reading at a fourth-grade level. The 1960s and the Right to Read movement gave growth and focus to Fay's efforts to build a nationally respected department. He envisioned the department as an umbrella covering phonics-based research and curricula and the newer sociolinguistic approach of whole language.

# History

## Another Milestone at I.U. As School Grows From Humble Beginning in 1820

By LOU EVON

Another milestone in the history of Indiana University is being marked today with the dedication of the $831,000 new wing of the Education Building. It is commemorated to the one-hundredth anniversary of teacher education on the I. U. campus.

To the casual observor, I.U. is "big," and has many buildings. But for a group of far-sighted men, the University would not have grown from a humble brick structure to an institution with more than 150 buildings and 850 acres of land. Today I.U. is a leader of Indiana's system of public education.

The University had its orgin on April 19, 1816 when an act of Congress provided for the admission of Indiana into the Union. In that act, the Federal government offered the new State a township of land for the "use of a seminary of learning." The convention which framed the Indiana Constitution declared that, "It shall be the duty of the General Assembly . . . to provide by law for a general system of education, ascending in a regular gradation from township schools to a State university, wherein tuition shall be gratis, and equally open to all." No other state in the Union had then incorporated into its constitution a declaration in favor of a university open to all with free tuition.

It is significant that Dr. David Maxwell, who drafted the clause of the Constitution excluding slavery from Indiana is regarded as the "founder of Indiana University." In the winter of 1819, Dr. Maxwell went on horseback to Corydon to lobby for the people of Bloomington to bring the seminary here. An act, which narrowly escaped defeat, was passed on January 20, 1820. That date is now recognized by the University as Founders Day. The act named a Board of Trustees to select a site for the seminary in the reserved township. The original site, now known as the Old College Campus, is located at the end of College avenue near the Bloomington High School annex.

Two buildings were constructed. One building was a professor's residence costing $891. The other was a "pretenious" two-story school building. It cost $2,400. The Indiana State Seminary first opened its doors May 1, 1824. Ten students enrolled and one professor was offered $250 a year to teach. The first professor, the Rev. Baynard R. Hall, was the only instructor from 1824 to 1827. The only subjects taught were Greek and Latin. In 1827 a second professor, John M. Harney, was added to the faculty.

**Seminary Changes to College.**

January 24, 1828, the General Assembly, upon a favorable report of the Board of Visitors, passed an act to raise the Seminary to the rank of a college. Gov. James B. Ray pressed the claims of the Seminary upon the legislature for state support. "Indiana College" was dedicated to the education of youth for the study of English, foreign languages, arts, sciences, and literature.

Dr. Andrew Wylie was elected the first president in 1829. In addition to his duties as president, Dr. Wylie taught "Moral and Mental Philosophy," and "Political Economy and Polite Literature." The College endowment in 1878 was nearly $40,000 with an annual income of $2,000. There were thirty-five students on campus, which consisted of ten acres. The street from College avenue to town was unpaved, and the sidewalk was a clay footpath.

By an act in February 25, 1838, Indiana College become Indiana University, with authority to grant additional degrees in law and medicine. The 1839 faculty consisted of three members, including the president. In the following year there were about sixty-four students.

**First State School for Women.**

In 1867 the University took a radical step when it became the first State university to admit women. Sarah Parke Morrison, not knowing that the Board of Trustees was considering admission of women, petitioned the Trustees to admit "females." She become the first coed among three hundred men students.

Of the two new buildings that were constructed in 1833, after a fire destroyed the buildings of the old University campus, both remain much the same as they were originally. After the fire I.U. moved to its present site to be away from the noise of the railroads. The site was known then as Dunn Woods.

Owen Hall was built on the new campus for the Department of Natural Science and the Museum. It was named in honor of Richard Owen, geologist and professor of natural science from 1863 to 1879. Wylie Hall was built for the Departments of Chemistry and Physics, and until 1888, it was used for the library and other departments.

**Maxwell Hall Completed in 1890.**

Maxwell Hall was completed in 1890 and was named in honor of Dr. David A. Maxwell, one of the most energetic developers of the State Seminary, and for his son, Dr. James D. Maxwell, '58, a member of the Board of Trustees from 1860 to 1892. Soon after completion of these three buildings, an expansion program resulted in the construction of Kirkwood Hall. Assembly Hall, a wooden structure erected east of Owen Hall in 1896, was used as a men's gymnasium and for convocations. It served that purpose until 1917, and was torn down in 1938.

Funds for the Student Building, built at a cost of $100,000 in 1906, were donated half by the students and friends of the University and half by John D. Rockerfeller. It served as the center of social life on the campus until the Union Building was built in 1932. Science Hall was dedicated in 1903 at the installation of Dr. William Lowe Bryan as president of the University. Biology Hall followed in construction in 1910. The Commerce Building was dedicated in 1923, but later the name was changed to the Business and Economics Building in 1931.

**Raise Funds for Stadium.**

In 1921, a resolution was passed by the I.U. Alumni Association to raise funds for a football stadium for the "Fighting Hoosiers." Immediately, an organization of students and faculty started the drive for funds, and thirty hours afterwards, they had raised $400,000, for three memorial buildings including the Union Building, Memorial Hall residence for women, and Memorial Stadium. Construction of the stadium was begun, and in November, 1925 it was dedicated to "those who have served the nation in the wars of the Republic."

Three years after the dedication of Memorial Stadium, the I.U. Fieldhouse was dedicated in December of 1928 with a game between the "Fighting Hoosiers" and the University of Pennsylvania. The cost of the fieldhouse was $350,000, and a percentage of the gate receipts was used to pay the cost of building. Later constructions include the Chemistry Building in 1931, the Administration Building and the School of Music in 1936, and the Medical Building in 1937. The Auditorium was built in 1941.

Shortly after the end of World War II, the enrollment at I.U. took a sharp increase. Many veterans began enrolling and the housing situation became critical. The first dormitory built to relieve this shortage was Rogers Center II. It was dedicated July 18, 1946. The center houses 1,000 men, and feeds 7,100 persons. The University Apartments for married couples were opened in 1949. The project was financed by a 2 million-dollar bond issue.

The last dormitory to be built was Men's New Hall, better known as the Men's Quad. Construction began in July, 1947 and was completed in the Fall of 1949.

Since the opening of Indiana University on May 1, 1824, it has grown from an enrollment of ten students to over 22,000 students with over 15,000 on campus. In its nine extension centers are found 7,000 students on a full time or part time basis.

*School of Education Dedication Section*

# THE INDIANA DAILY STUDENT

# 100-Year Story of Progress— The I. U. School of Education

—DAILY STUDENT PHOTO By BERNARD HANLEY
DISCUSS BUILDING PLANS — Dean Wendell W. Wright, of the School of Education, talks over plans for the new wing with Dr. Paul Seagers, right, school building consultant for the University.

## Revisions and Set Backs Plague Building 12 Years

By DICK ALLEN

The new Education Building was originally planned in 1937 as a wing of University School. At that time it would have cost approximately $250,000. When the building was actually finished in the Spring of 1949, it had cost $831,000.

The original plans were discarded because the Indiana Legislature said the cost was too high. In 1940, under pressure of a rapidly increasing staff, Henry Lester Smith, then Dean of the School of Education, had the plans revised and put before the Legislature. Again the projected building plans had to be discarded—"the cost is too high."

The plans were again revised in 1942 because of a still increasing School of Education staff. This time the war and its resultant material and labor shortages caused the proposed plans for the new building to be abandoned.

**Wright Pushes Work.**

After the war Wendell W. Wright was made Dean of the School and he again began to work for a revision of plans and the completion of the new building.

In 1947, Dean Wright called in Dr. Paul Seagers, now school building planning consultant and associate professor of education, to again revise the plans in view of the ever-increasing needs for more space and facilities for the School of Education.

**Construction Begins.**

During the 1949 session the Indiana Legislature allowed the appropriation, and building was begun in October of the same year. With the exception of a few minor strikes and labors shortages, construction went forward smoothly until the wing was finished in the Spring of 1951.

Architects for the Bloomington limestone building were McGuire and Shook, of Indianapolis, and the general contractors were Johnson, Drake and Piper. The I. U. co-ordinating architect was E. P. Bardwell while Dr. Seagers was the liason man who worked in close co-operation with the original architects.

**Schools Together.**

The original intention in adding the new wing was to have the School of Education and the practice school together. In spite of a total of 52,705 square feet the needs of the School of Education have cut into the amount of space which was to be allowed University School. However, there are still eleven new classrooms, four laboratories, three seminar rooms, thirty-eight instructors' offices and a library reading room containing 3,805 square feet.

The entire building was planned, furnished, and decorated through the co-operative study and participation of the members of the faculty of the School of Education. Particular attention was paid to the function of every area as making the entire building a comfortable and wholesome environment.

### 19 Parts Now One

Dean W. W. Wright, of the School of Education, said that in the past, the School of Education has had to spread its classes through nineteen buildings on the campus. Now it is all in one building which has been built for the purpose, and has all of the latest laboratory materials available.

**SPECIAL PERFORMANCE.**

A special performance of "A Murder Has Been Arranged" will be given tonight by the Brown County players at the theatre in Nashville. Members of Phi Delta Kappa and the textbook exhibitors will attend.

**ARCHITECTS FOR WING.**

Architects for the new Bloomington limestone wing of the Education building were McQuire and Shook of Indianapolis, and the General contractors were Johnson, Drake, and Piper.

## From 34 Students in 1851 Comes Leading Institution

By DORIS M. BROWN

The story of the School of Education is a story of progress.

From a class of didactics of thirty-four students organized Oct. 4, 1851 has grown a school with an enrollment of approximately three thousand persons.

Dr. Andrew Wylie was president of I.U. when the Board of Trustees asked that a class in didactics be organized "including the theory and practice of teaching, with a view to the permanent establishment of a Normal Department in connection with the University."

Dr. Wylie died a month later, but with his successor, Alfred Ryors, came the enactment from the General Assembly, on June 17, 1852, that a Normal Department be established by the trustees.

In the Fall Daniel Read became the first I.U. professor of didactics and John Calvin Smith the teacher of the "Model School." Twenty-fourt males and twelve females enrolled.

Between 1857 and 1885, there were periods when the program was suspended. When David Starr Jordan became President of the University in 1885, teacher training was resumed with Prof. William Lowe Bryan then, acting professor of philosophy, teaching three courses.

**Department of Pedagogy.**

1886 saw teacher training work established into a Department of Pedagogy with Richard G. Boone as professor of pedagogics.

According to Prof. Boone's records, by 1890 the work had expanded into eleven courses reaching one-fourth of the student body.

The year of 1891 was auspicious, for it was then that "education" was recognized as a major subject. That year eight students were graduated with a major in pedagogics. The next year heralded extension courses in Louisville and Evansville.

The first course in "Psychology and Pedagogy" was offered in the summer of 1895. When in 1894, Dr. Bryan became the professor in charge, John A. Bergstrom became assistant professor and set up a Pedagogical Museum.

**Becomes Department.**

Dr. Bergstrom took over pedagogical duties when Dr. Bryan became president of the University in 1902. Under his leadership pedagogy became the Department of Education in 1904.

Two years later observation and practice teaching in elementary and secondary schools appeared. The next year three critic teachers were employed.

Effective Aug. 1, 1908, was the General Assembly provision that twelve weeks of professional training be given beginning teachers. The catalog reports 189, students the first year the department was erected into the School of Education with Dr. Bryan as dean.

**Received A.B.**

Students were admitted through the College of Arts and did not take the professional course until the sophomore year. Graduates received the A.B. degree with a major in education for which forty-five term hours in education were required.

The school continued growing between 1911 and 1916 when Walter A. Jessup, W.W. Black, and Henry Lester Smith were the successive deans. In 1916 twenty-five courses were offered.

It was a further sign of progress when County examinations for teachers were abolished and licenses were issued on a basis of training in 1923. A year later the School received the right to confer its own degrees. The first B.S. degree in education was granted October, 1925, to one candidate.

**Graduate Division.**

Since 1929, the School of Education has maintained a graduate division. The first M.S. in Education was granted three candidates that year, and the first doctor of education degree three years later to two students.

The 1930's brought licensing of public health nurses and school librarians. The master's degree became compulsory for a license as an administrator in 1935. The decade of the '30's saw the creation of the Physical Welfare Department. The Bureau of Teacher Recommendation was organized in 1936.

With the opening of the University School on the campus in 1938 came the opportunity for students in education to complete graduate training without leaving the Campus.

**Abandon Course.**

At the turn of the decade elementary licenses were given on four years of training only, the two-year normal course having been abandoned in 1937.

Dr. Wendell W. Wright, on the staff since 1925, became Dean of the School of Education in 1946. It was that year that the School of Health, Physical Education, and Recreation was formed and took over all related courses originally in the School of Education.

The School of Education now offers courses covering the entire field of teacher training. It has full equality with other professional schools of the University.

**School Surveys.**

Under the sponsorship of the School of Education, school surveys are made, and conferences and workshops given on educational problems. Outstanding among the School publications are the Bulletin of the School of Education, the School Survey Series, and the Nursing Education Monographs.

The Division of Research and Field Services works in co-operation with the schools in dealing with problems vital to the efficiency of the public schools of the State.

The story of the School of Education has been a story of progress.

### Dean Wright Author Of Several Books

Some of the books Dean W. W. Wright, of the School of Education, has written are Twentieth Century Speller, 1927; Practical Arithmetic Workbook, 1928; Development and Use of Indiana Composite Achievement Tests, 1929; Tests and Measurements (with H. L. Smith), 1929; Modern Day Readers, 1934; Work and Play with Words (with Nell Parkinson), 1936; co-author of Our Developing Civilization (a series of social studies textbooks), 1937; A Letter to Grandmother, 1941; The Navajoes, 1942, and Survey of Louisville Public Schools (with others), 1943.

—DAILY STUDENT PHOTO By BERNARD HANLEY
DEAN WRIGHT AND "CREW" — Mrs. Dorothy McCaw, administrative assistant to Dean Wendell W. Wright, of the School of Education, and Mrs. James (Angie) Wrenn, secretary, (standing), discuss plans for today's cedication program with Dean Wright in the Dean's private office in the new wing of the Education Building.

## Picture of Dean Wright— 'A True Education Leader'

By G. M. HAGGARD

Dean Wendell William Wright, of the School of Education, is one of the few really modest men left in the world. His associates are only too glad to tell about their boss, however, and a picture of the man shows a true leader in the field of education.

Dean Wright, as noted from casual observation, is a hard worker—a terribly hard worker. He will push his associates to the limit but they will never work harder than he himself. In his dealings with others, he is scrupulously fair. No one can truthfully say he ever got a "raw deal" from the head of the School of Education.

From the man himself, no reason for the fact that he is time and again picked for top positions in the field of education would ever be heard. A little investigation reveals that Dr. Wright's keen mind is the one which always gets to the problem and brings out the essential issues in committee work. His keen insight is valuable in any meeting.

**Talks of Hopes.**

One thing Dean Wright does talk about is his hopes and aspirations—not for himself—but for the cause of education and the University as a whole. His main interest is in education and the way in which he can improve its service to the community. He can talk at great lengths about the School of Education and its many accomplishments without taking any personal credit.

The Dean wants the School to continue its well-balanced basis in elementary and secondary teaching, and the special fields such as music and physical education. He said the undergraduate division, as well as the graduate division, which now has the largest enrollment in its history, now gives I.U. one of the largest and finest teacher training centers in the country.

**Graduate Division.**

The graduate division of the School of Education has grown tremendously since the end of the war, and Dean Wright wants to keep it in pace with the rest of the University graduate divisions.

He also said the school is extending its services through the establishment this year of the new Institute of Educational Research which deals with long-range planning.

Dean Wright expressed appreciation of the fact that the University wanted the School of Education to have this new building. He considers it a tribute to the services performed by the School.

**Many Honors.**

Many honors have come to Dean Wright in his long and productive career as one of the nation's top educators. National, State, and local organizations have recognized his abilities as an administrator and "idea man" with membership on many important positions on commissions and committees.

Among the positions he holds or has held are member of the Standards Committee of the American Association of Colleges for Teacher Education; member of the National Commission on Life Adjustment (appointed by the U. S. Office of Education); secretary of the Indiana Conference of Higher Education; director of the State School Facilities Survey, and, his latest job, director of Administrative Studies and Institutional Relations.

Dr. Wright is also well-known as an author, especially in the field of elementary education. The book of which he is most proud is probably "The Rainbow Dictionary," published in 1947. This book, with the aid of pictures, gives the basic words of a child's vocabulary in a clear and concise form.

**Indiana Product.**

Dean Wright is, in his own words, a product of the Indiana public school system. He was born in Greencastle and attended schools in Indiana until he received the A.B. degree from Indiana State Teachers College in 1916. He did some Summer work at the University of Colorado and the University of Chicago and received the Ph.D. degree from Teachers College, Columbia University, in 1929.

He immediately returned to In-

(Continued on Page Four)

## Efficiency! Management!

### Mrs. McCaw and 'Angie' Help Dean.

The harmony and smoothness with which the School of Education runs is due in large measure to the efficient management of Mrs. Dorothy McCaw, Dean Wendell W. Wright's administrative assistant.

A veteran of eight years of Dean Wright's many moves and offices, she is firmly convinced that she holds the best job in the world.

If you've a gripe about the way classes are arranged, see Mrs. McCaw. Maybe you're looking for a job in the School of Education—see Mrs. McCaw. If the School has a tea or any other large social function and you want to get the real low-down—see Mrs. McCaw.

In other words, if you have a question pertaining to the School of Education, Mrs. McCaw has the answer and is glad to hand it out.

Dean Wright, being a busy man, sometimes has no use for buzzers and phones. He prefers to use his more than ample voice. One of the calls most frequently heard is that of, "ANGIE!"

Angie—Mrs. James C. Wrenn—is Dean Wright's personable and efficient secretary. She has worked with Dean Wright since August, 1950. As she puts it, her main job is "keeping track of the Dean."

She attended Northwestern University for two years before coming here with her husband, a senior in the School of Health, Physical Education, and Recreation.

Angie is an excellent secretary—courteous, poised, and helpful—and keeps track of Dean Wright with efficiency and tact.

## 'Color,' Explains Dr. Paul Seagers, 'It's Color That Does It'

By RUTH BOONE

Dr. Paul W. Seagers, associate professor of education and nationally recognized school building consultant, snapped on a light in a small room near his office in the new School of Education Building.

The room appeared to be a poorly lighted closet. Dr. Seagers turned to a similar room adjoining the first and flipped on the light there. The difference was unbelievable. Here was a perfectly lighted room exactly like the first —except for one thing.

"Color," said Dr. Seagers, "It is color that does it; the kind and amount of light is identical in each room, but the walls of the first one are painted black and the walls of the second are painted yellow."

Dr. Seagers explained that these are demonstration rooms used to illustrate objectively what is meant by color dynamics.

The delicate tint on the walls and ceiling of the second room reflects the light and makes it work, while the black paint in the first room absorbs the light and kills it; therefore, although the light available from the fixture is the same, one room is dark, the other light.

The entrance-way gives visitors a clue to the particularly pleasing color schemes found throughout the building. Here the walls are a dark rose above panels of Colorado marble. This shade was blended especially to pick up and accentuate the rosy tints in the marble.

The color schemes in the building are based on four tints, yellow, green, blue, and peach, plus two accent shades, Monterey red and Wedgewood blue.

A number of things had to be considered before final combinations for individual rooms were decided.

"Wherever possible, the professor who was to occupy the room was consulted and given an opportunity to choose the colors," said Dr. Seagers, "and after that we had to consider light and depth of vision.

"We usually applied the accent shade to the wall farthest away to bring it closer," explained Dr. Seagers, "and the other walls received the tint."

Each room is set up on a definite formula; the ceilings must reflect 80 per cent of the light that hits them, the walls 60 per cent, and the furniture and floors from 40 to 60 per cent.

Even sky-brightness was taken into consideration as a contrast to surfaces around the inside of windows.

The walls of Dean Wright's office are a combination of Monterey red and creamy yellow. The furniture is bleached walnut upholstered in light green and dark blue leather. The ceiling is white acoustical tile, as are the ceilings in the building.

"Normally, yellow is a good color for a north exposure," said Dr. Seagers, speaking of the Records Room, "but here, where accuracy is of prime importance, we used green to keep the typists cool and calm."

Green and blue were used in the interviewing rooms because of the restful effect of these colors.

Woodwork throughout the building is light oak finished with a dull surface. Dr. Seagers explained that such non-glare surfaces make the light in the room more efficient.

The Library Reference Room is especially charming and restful where walls are finished in peach and the large pillars down the center in Wedgewood blue.

Dr. Seagers' favorite combination is in a classroo mwhere two tints are combined, peach on three walls and green on the fourth.

Special section from the July 1951 issue of the *Indiana Daily Student*.

At midcentury, more students were enrolled in distance and extension courses than were resident in Bloomington. A significant proportion of those students were teacher education majors. The development of A-V materials, often tested in the University School, opened doors to a new virtual classroom. Many extension and distance education students were adults. Midwest Airborne Television Instruction ("The Flying Classroom"), a precursor to satellites, flew over cities and broadcast courses on TV. Working quietly but steadily on behalf of teaching and learning, A-V technology was now a powerhouse. It would be fully integrated into the school with the formation of the Division of Instructional Systems Technology in 1972 when Larson retired and Mendel Sherman became director. Who could have anticipated a trajectory from A-V to AI?

Academic programs and departments grew apace. The school calved off other disciplines (nursing; library science; health, physical education, and recreation) while drawing closer to core functions of the university. In 1959, after much wrangling, the school joined the University Division of Graduate Studies. The Department of Counseling and Guidance (now the Department of Counseling and Educational Psychology) tripled in size under Paul Munger, chairman of the department in 1963. Using training and research grants from the US Department of Labor and Office of Education, Munger recruited a cadre of scholars who produced top national rankings for two generations, particularly in school counseling. By the mid-1970s, School of Education faculty had doubled in size to approximately 200 full-time professors.

During these heady years of growth, many faculty were spending as much time as grant administrators and researchers as teachers, a paradigm that became a norm. Anabel Newman created the Reading Practicum Center and directed it for over 20 years. Philip G. Smith enlarged the Department of Historical, Philosophical, and Comparative Studies in Education and wrote his groundbreaking *Reflective Thinking: The Method of Education,* with Gordon Hullfish. Fay Arganbright directed the Bureau of Educational Placement on her way to national recognition as a leader in educational placement. Clinton Chase joined the Department of Educational Psychology and developed the university's first electronically scored student rating of faculty, known as Multi-Op. John Leblanc arrived in 1968 to become a national authority in elementary mathematics teacher education. With money from the National Science Foundation, he established the Mathematics Education Development Center, hired 20 employees, and held summer programs around the country.

Shirley Engle was instrumental in establishing the Social Studies Development Center in 1968 and earned a national reputation in social studies education and curriculum theory. In 1970 Robert Gibson and Marianne Mitchell initiated Indiana University's Scotland Program and in 1972 its Bermuda Program, establishing counseling and counselor education programs in both countries while offering academic credit to IU students in a variety of disciplines. Both programs functioned until 2000. Martha Dawson, who received her master's and doctoral degrees from the School of Education, moved back to Bloomington in 1970 to accept a position as professor of education. She developed a multicultural education program in the school and was the first African American woman to become a tenured member of the IU Bloomington faculty. James D. Anderson, an African American professor of education, arrived shortly thereafter.

Robert Gibson and Marianne Mitchell (far left) and Pat Ryan and President Ryan (far right) in Scotland to establish counseling and counselor education programs.

Relatives of Martha Dawson at her portrait unveiling in 2022.

Martha Dawson.

International activities flourished. From 1960 through 1971, the School of Education launched elementary, secondary, and/or higher education projects in Pakistan, Sierra Leone, Uruguay, Saudi Arabia, and Chile. James Mahan, who joined the school in 1971 as director of the professional year, began discussions to expand the program into Native American and Latino communities, laying groundwork for today's award-winning Global Gateway for Teachers.

Campus ferment was a staple of American campuses at the time, and Indiana University was no exception. In 1968 the school established a Human Relations Commission to address student concerns. Graduate and undergraduate student advisory boards followed. In 1969 Dean Clark invited students to "sit in" and air their grievances. As a result, the school formed a Commission on Teacher Education that included students.

Drawing of the Center for Human Growth original location.

Photo of the Center for Human Growth original location taken in 2023.

In 1970 Alan Bell, Kinsey Institute psychologist and professor in the Department of Counseling and Guidance, was first director of the Center for Human Growth, housed in a brick house with a porch swing on Eighth Street near campus. In June 1971 the school's Policy Council authorized a Division of Teacher Education committed to "self-renewal and growth," bywords of the era.[40] In November of that year Dean Clark urged that "research, development, and training in teacher education be broadened substantially."[41] He encouraged faculty creativity and greater involvement of students.

Largely in response to student agitation, teacher education underwent reform. Self-actualization and human growth were new terms that accented the institutional lexicon. Voices of students were being heard. The Division of Teacher Education began in 1972, funded by an HEW grant. Leo Fay was its first director. David Clark had asked James Mahan to expand the professional year program in response to student demands for racial and ethnic diversity.

Despite unrest and confrontation, research never faltered. In fact, it took inspiration from the times. The human growth and potential movement of the 1960s began to characterize the counseling curriculum and counseling faculty research, laying the ground for the social justice and student-centered orientation of today's Department of Counseling and Educational Psychology.

Fittingly named for its longest serving dean and longtime director of the Bureau of Cooperative Research, the Smith Research Center opened in 1973 in space reconfigured from the University School at 10th and the Bypass. Funded programs moved there as did departments of educational psychology, and counseling and guidance.

Aerial view of the University School complex in 1964.

The University School library in 1964.

The golden era emerged as much from crucible as cradle. After 43 years of the same two deans and presidents, the school had four deans and five university presidents in 15 years. Given the contrast between constancy and change, student pranking and social unrest, it is surprising that a golden era dawned for the school. To the credit of visionary individuals and support from federal programs, the school flourished instead of floundered. No era, of course, is only golden. There were very few Black faculty in the school, and many more men than women on the faculty. Half the faculty was on "soft" money (from grants), and many were spread over campus in centers and institutes, inhibiting community. Still, a culture of multidisciplinary, groundbreaking research took hold in a 15-year span of time.

Strong presidential leadership complemented the school's achievements. Elvis Stahr became president of IU in 1962. Widely praised for strong government and academic credentials, he proved a worthy successor to Herman Wells. Stahr kept the promise of academic freedom, inherited from his predecessor. He converted extension systems of Northwest, South Bend, and Ft. Wayne campuses into four-year, degree-granting colleges. Teacher education fueled enrollment on those campuses. He helped IU professors gain administrative posts and teaching positions around the world.

By the end of Stahr's presidency, IU had a 52% increase in Bloomington enrollment and a 50.9% increase across all campuses. In 1968, one-third of all university students (47,642) were on regional campuses or the Indianapolis campus.[42] Such growth foreshadowed even greater regional campus development under soon-to-be President John Ryan, an IU alumnus.[43] Stahr greatly advanced the already-expansive portfolio of international programs and partnerships of the university. The unrest of the 1960s took its toll, however. Elvis Stahr left the university thoroughly exhausted at the end of a six-year term.

Few education deans could have been more instrumental than David Clark. He provided invaluable advice to faculty in preparing grants for federal funding. He championed research at every level. He anticipated student malaise and wove it into the fabric of the institution. He led reform of teacher education and oversaw the establishment of a student leadership institute. He restructured divisions in the school and created cooperative programs of doctoral degrees, a commission on women, and a division of teacher education. He engineered the transition of the University School to the Monroe County Community School Corporation and hired its teachers. He appointed 125 faculty in eight years.

Partnering with the School of Public and Environmental Affairs, Clark established a National Center for Public Choice in Education. He began work on President Ryan's task force to study the feasibility of merging the schools of education in Indianapolis and Bloomington. He was responsible for 29 research centers and institutes and helped secure funding for all of them. Not a glad-hander, more often at the edges of a national conference room than in the middle, he embodied the highest ideals of knowledge generation. Clark believed in the problem-solving virtue of research, which for him meant the best sense of development.

In 1970 Indiana University celebrated its 150th birthday. The institution had come a long way from its backwoods origins as a frontier seminary. Bloomington had electricity now and paved roads. Students lived in dormitories instead of boarding houses. There was more to do on the Courthouse Square than pull up your horse, sit on a bench, whistle, and whittle. Faculty and presidents were increasingly graduates of the university, no longer imported from the East Coast. World War I had opened the doors of the campus to the world. After World War II, the university walked through those doors into a world it was helping to shape. The university was now an international leader in educational partnerships, research, and technology. Tens of thousands of students were studying in Bloomington and on regional campuses across the state. Hundreds of millions of dollars filled the budget.

Herman B Wells speaking at the Founder's Day Program in May 1970 celebrating the University's 150th anniversary.

Changes in the School of Education were equally dramatic. It had become the premier teacher education institution in the state and a leading research school in the country. It graduated school psychologists, educational psychologists, and counselors. It provided educational leadership to schools, private industry, and universities around the world. It enjoyed unprecedented enrollments.

At the 150th birthday dinner of Indiana University, Chancellor Herman B Wells called for civility among colleagues. He said that at its best the university "is a place for disciplined thought, the custodian of our culture, and the center of that intellectual concern and unrest which can change the world."[44] William Lynch, chairman of the Department of Educational Psychology from 1955 to 1968, took Wells's blueprint one step further when he wrote, "A university has a special responsibility to society for intellectual rigor and dependable contributions."[45] The golden era of the School of Education had fulfilled Wells's and Lynch's ideals of a university. As in the business cycle, however, bust was lurking around the corner from boom.

The golden era did not survive for long in the 1970s. The end of post-World War II and Great Society expansion was a blow to the campus, as the university had benefited from the school's enrollment and growth. Throughout the new era, however, the school remained the largest producer of new teachers in Indiana. Nonetheless, the end of the era was instructive: It left the school with powerful insights about ways research can enrich teaching and service.

The vastly different landscape that greeted the school in the economic downturn of the mid-1970s was not just a matter of the federal goose no longer laying golden eggs. Within several years, a new national administration wanted to get rid of the Department of Education. The school and nation faced the declaration of a national educational emergency in 1983 when the National Commission on Excellence in Education published *A Nation at Risk: The Imperative for Educational Reform*. Instead of growth, there were cuts in faculty ranks from 200 to 140 full-time education faculty, new leadership of school and university, school faculty splintered across campus, and faltering morale. Herman Wells's and William Lynch's vision of education as cultural custodian, center of intellectual rigor, civil discourse, and change, and helpmate of society would be tested in the next two decades.

# CHAPTER 4

# A Nation at Risk, a School at Work (1974–1991)

The 1970s began expansively and ended in retrenchment. At the beginning of the decade, the benefits of Great Society programs were still being felt. As the war in Vietnam ended, students refocused on the classroom. Baby boomers who had flooded universities as undergraduates were now in graduate schools. Research funding had not dried up yet. The first generation of Peace Corps volunteers were assistant professors of education forming departments of international studies. Educational technology stepped out of A-V shops to join the academic mainstream in newly fashioned departments.

In 1981, however, a new national administration found government the problem, not the solution. Federal funding for education was already waning when the National Commission on Excellence in Education published its headline-grabbing *A Nation at Risk: The Imperative for Educational Reform*.

President Ronald Reagan addresses a meeting of teachers and administrators in Washington from outstanding secondary schools across the nation on August 27, 1984.

The report was a bold rebuke of the status quo in American schools, warning against the "rising tide of mediocrity that threatens our very future as a Nation and a people."[46] Given the popularity of the publication, not all education proposals went unfunded. By the end of the decade, the School of Education had piggybacked the concept of excellence in an equally bold move to win broad support for a new building.

It must be said that *A Nation at Risk* was not received uncritically. Among educationists, one critic was Donald Warren, who would become dean of the School of Education in 1990. His book, written with two colleagues, lamented the unrealistic educational reports of the early 1980s. Their critique appears later in this chapter. *A Nation at Risk* linked failure of American schools with erosion of the country's technology, industry, science, and commerce. By making that charge, however, the report opened the door to a marriage of technology and education. It was a door that Howard Mehlinger, who would later be named dean of the school, walked through.

Howard Mehlinger at his desk.

By careful management and strategic outreach, the school did more with less. Economic times were difficult, but the school persevered. Faculty reformed teacher education and continued to conduct research. Counseling and psychology expanded their curricula. Partnerships with Indiana schools and international universities leveraged tight dollars. Despite charges in *A Nation at Risk* that American education was idling, two education professors and their teams were doing anything but idling.

One of the most innovative projects of its generation was a 20-year research and development program conceived by educational psychologists David Gliessman and Richard Pugh. Their award-winning, paradigm-changing research integrated A-V technology, skills as concepts, and teacher training. Also during this period, the school provided leadership and innovation to corporations and policymakers via instructional systems and consulting. By the end of the 1980s, the ink was all but dry on a contract for a new, multimillion-dollar education building with state-of-the-art technology. The deal was brilliantly struck with federal, state, corporate, and university support at a time of government retrenchment.

The 1971 inauguration of John Ryan as president of Indiana University stabilized the presidency after the unexpected resignation of Joseph Sutton and the one-year return of Herman Wells. Ryan, a political scientist, served 14 years in office and retired in 1987, the fourth longest serving president. His most significant accomplishments were the strengthening of regional campuses and the expansion of international programs, two areas in which the School of Education played a leading role. Teacher education was the anchor of regional enrollment, and the school was a prolific contractor with overseas partners.

Richard P. Gousha, dean of the school from 1974 to 1980, took over from David Clark. As federal funding ran out, faculty on "soft" grant money returned to salaried lines, joined by new hires with tenure from the University School. Income was down, enrollment was down, expenses were up, and cuts were inevitable. After Clark's optimistic boom times, Gousha inherited the bust. "Saddled" with the task of merging education faculties in Indianapolis and Bloomington, he "spent his entire tenure slashing the School of Education budget."[47] Replacing Gousha in 1980 as acting dean was the widely respected Laurence D. Brown, educational psychologist and associate dean of academic affairs. A year later, Howard D. Mehlinger became dean. He was the man for the moment.

Richard Gousha.

Laurence Brown.

Historian by training, Mehlinger directed the school's Social Studies Development Center, established by Clark, before starting his nine-year term as dean. "Unlike David Clark," Mehlinger reflected, "I had no overarching vision of what the School could or should become."[48] Mehlinger did have, however, the glad hand that Clark lacked. Bringing together Congress, private industry, the state of Indiana, and Indiana University, Howard Mehlinger raised $30 million for the building that the school now occupies.

One example of Mehlinger's glad hand was his encounter with official decorum in the dean's office when he arrived. "Everyone had been on a first name basis in my Center," he wrote. "But the dean's office was very formal. First thing I needed to do was get the stiffness out of the office. My secretary would say, 'Would the Dean like some coffee?' And I would say, 'Yes, the Dean would.'"[49] It took a while, but formalities ceased.

The School of Education had pivotal leadership when it needed it—whether President William Lowe Bryan, who as acting dean secured the school in 1908, Henry Lester Smith and Wendell Wright, who advanced the school's professional credentials, David L. Clark, who raised funds and frontiers for research and development, Howard Mehlinger, who built a world-class building, or Donald Warren, who hired half the faculty during his 10-year tenure and remade the school with topflight appointments.

Despite a leaner time than the golden era, the mid-1970s to early 1990s was still a period of progress for the school. A partial list of accomplishments belies the difficult economic times: outstanding research programs, inauguration of a transformative cultural immersion project for student teaching, major private endowment of faculty and graduate student research, establishment of education policy centers, creation of a "core campus" that linked Bloomington and Indianapolis schools of education, daring and principled reforms of teacher education, approval of a counseling psychology program, strong national rankings for instructional technology,

IUB Education Dean Howard Mehlinger and IUPUI Education Dean Hugh Wolf at the dedication of the new Indianapolis building in 1982.

and a breakthrough engagement with mainland China highlighted a challenging era.

During this time, instructional technology transitioned from an A-V education program to a department. Its restructuring incorporated cultural perspectives and behaviorist objectives envisioned in Robert Gagné's *The Conditions of Learning*. After a segmented curriculum with A-V products in one course and psychology in another, the Department of Instructional Systems Technology (IST) wove together analysis, evaluation, assessment, and theory in a single course with a project-based approach. Instructional consulting won contracts with Eli Lilly and Company and AT&T. A corporate master's program placed scores of graduates with Lilly alone, as well as in China and Malaysia. IST was not dominated by any one discipline at this time, although corporate ties ceased being a focus as the department developed.

From 1971 through 1975 David Gliessman directed the National Center for the Development of Training Materials in Teacher Education, funded by a grant from the US Office of Education. The Center launched a 20-year groundbreaking research program on the acquisition of teaching skills through concept-based training. The Gliessman and Pugh collaboration is an example of the visionary research in the school at this time.

Teaching pedagogical skills as concepts with protocol films for illustration and interpretation was a new approach in 1971. The enterprise attracted a multidisciplinary cadre of veteran and rising stars in the school who included educational psychologists Laurence D. Brown, Clinton Chase, Gary Ingersoll, and Richard Turner; and professors Lee Ehman (Department of Secondary Education–Social Studies), Howard Levie

(Division of Instructional Systems Technology), James Oakey (Department of Science Education), Philip Smith (Department of Historical, Philosophical, and Comparative Studies), and James Walden (Department of Elementary Education–Language Arts).

Gliessman and Pugh's center had four principal activities: development and distribution of teacher-training materials, communication among developers and users of materials, formal and informal testing of materials during development, and in-service training in the use and development of teacher-training materials. The genius of their research was the translation of skills into concepts. Counterintuitively, their chief finding was that a trainee's command of the use and quality of a teaching skill related more closely to recognizing and interpreting the concept than practicing the skill. Once the concept was understood, the skill could be customized to meet particulars of situation and individual. Practice extended the skill cognitively but understanding the skill's concept determined mastery. Skill-concept pairs included productive and reproductive questioning, probing, informing, approving, and disapproving.

Products of the center were self-instructional manuals, audiotapes, and filmstrips. The school's highly developed A-V Center and its instructional systems technology division played an essential role in storing a wide range of teaching excerpts (or protocols) on videodisc; rapidly and flexibly accessing excerpts to provide multiple skill examples; and permitting interaction of instructor or trainee with examples of matching concept characteristics with skills. Supported by protocol films, the strategic selection of concepts and their clear definition and demonstration as skills proved consequential to teacher education.

The center was a five-year project. Beyond the products of the center, the 20-year collaboration yielded 39 national reports, conference papers, or published articles in *Journal of Educational Psychology*, *Journal of Teacher Education*, *Review of Educational Research*, *International Journal of Educational Research*, *Journal of the Association of Teacher Education*, *Journal of Education for Teaching*, and *AV Communication Review*. The culmination of their pioneering interdisciplinary collaboration was the Harold E. Mitzell Award for Meritorious Contribution to Educational Practice Through Research, given to David Gliessman and Richard Pugh in 1994 from the *Journal of Educational Research* for their article, "Concept and Skill Relationships in a Teacher Training Setting."

The School of Education was advancing on many fronts despite a stretched budget and downturn in the national economy. Cultural immersion for student teachers was one such front. From 1971 to 1985 James Mahan, director of the professional year, who retired as emeritus professor of education, administered Project Options for Student Teachers (POST). The program began with Native American reservations, branched out to overseas placements, and is now Global Gateway for Teachers. It has won seven national awards for administration and worldwide outreach on behalf of student teachers.

Art education was building a strong foundation. Gilbert Clark and Enid Zimmerman joined Guy Hubbard on the faculty. The three would bring the department to national prominence in the mid-1990s. Clark developed an innovative curricular framework for teaching and learning about art, and Zimmerman helped set an agenda for research in the field. Clark and Zimmerman became national experts on education of artistically talented students.

In 1976, the school was ranked second or seventh, depending on which criterion was used to determine research standing among schools of education.[50] Myrtle Scott, associate professor of educational psychology, founded the Interdisciplinary Doctoral Program on Young Children, which she directed from

1972 to 1978. A theorist of child development and ecological psychology, Scott was the first Herman B Wells Endowed Professor, awarded in 2000, and became a leader protecting intellectual property rights of faculty.

As UNESCO senior expert in educational techniques and consultant for the Agency for International Development, Hans O. Andersen, professor of science education, worked in Thailand, South Africa, Pakistan, and new Guinea from 1972 to 1974. In 1974 Robert L. Wolf founded and directed the Indiana Center for Evaluation. The same year saw the completion of the merger of the schools of education in Bloomington and Indianapolis, helping to protect teacher education accreditation on the Indianapolis campus. In 1975 the Division of Instructional Systems Technology was listed as first choice of educational technology programs in *Change* magazine in a poll of US deans of schools of education.

Spurring research and outreach in the school was national legislation in 1975 to guarantee free appropriate public education suited to individual needs of the handicapped in a least restrictive environment. Ellen Brantlinger, professor of special education, community activist, and qualitative methodologist, began a 12-year series of 50 workshops and presentations on sexuality, disability, and the Americans with Disabilities Act. Brantlinger later chaired the Department of Special Education and helped the program transition to the Department of Curriculum and Instruction. In 1977 Leonard Burrello, associate professor of educational leadership, founded the National Inservice Network, advancing an inclusion model for special education.

The school returned to departmental organization in 1978 with 11 departments (administration and administrative studies; art education; counseling and guidance; curriculum and instruction; educational psychology; historical, philosophical, and comparative studies in education; instructional systems technology; language education; mathematics, science, and social studies; special education; vocational education, adult education, business education, distributive education, and home economics).

Consolidations have streamlined the school's departments to four today (curriculum and instruction; counseling and educational psychology; educational leadership and policy studies; and learning, design, and adult education). Learning, design, and adult education is a long way from the A-V Center, although World War II technology was crucial to adult education. In many ways the new departmental name for IST reflects a historic mission with an emphasis on design and learning science. Internally, contracting and expanding from courses in didactics and pedagogy to a department within a school to a school with its own departments, the School of Education has been like a breathing organism adapting to terrain and maturation. Externally, adjustment to social and political exigencies, leading while following, has been a hallmark of the school's successful struggles.

History and growth coincided in 1979 when the education building was renamed the Wendell W. Wright School of Education Building. Three decades earlier at the 1951 dedication of the education building at Third and Jordan (now Eagleson), an extension of the old University School, Wendell Wright had said that we shape our buildings and they shape us. Technology shaped the building that again bears his name today.

Herman B Wells, Dean Richard Gousha, and IU Vice President Robert O'Neil with Wendell W. Wright's daughters.

Architects and interior designers continue to fit that space to contemporary needs. The new education library, plans for the atrium, and a refurbished Center for Human Growth, among other projects, will contribute to greater comfort, efficiency, and community.

The 1980s began with a new dean, new summer offerings, a new award for faculty and graduate student dissertations (thanks to a generous gift from Maris and Mary Proffitt), and the dedication of the new Indiana University–Purdue University Indianapolis (IUPUI) School of Education. Fresh on the job, Dean Howard Mehlinger wrote to Egon Guba, associate dean until the mid-1970s, that the school needed a "better sense of purpose and direction with respect to research activity, especially collaborative research activity."[51] One of those initiatives was CARE (Center for Applied Research in Education). Team research was an ideal at the time. At his retirement from the school in 1996, Sam Guskin, who did most of his work with others, offered an ironic alternative: "As important as collaborative research is, there is an awful lot you can do by yourself."[52]

In 1981 Rex Stockton and Keith Morran in the counseling departments at Bloomington and IUPUI launched a 36-year, award-winning research program on the therapeutic factors of interpersonal verbal feedback in small groups. Findings in "The Use of Verbal Feedback in Counseling Groups: Toward an Effective System," published in the *Journal for Specialists in Group Work*, launched multiple studies over many years, dozens of conference presentations, national leadership positions, and a Chancellor's Professorship for Stockton in 2003. Experimental subjects for Stockton and Morran's investigations were drawn from counseling groups at the Center for Human Growth, the school's campus/community counseling center. The two researchers said they probably had more groups for their studies than anyone in the country. Stockton was one of the first of his generation to maintain a counseling research program rather than produce one-shot studies. He excelled at finding theory in the data. His discoveries advanced the therapeutic efficacy of small groups and produced a popular series of videotapes to train group-therapy leaders. His work was recognized by leadership and fellowship status in professional organizations of his field, award-winning mentorship, and by a 2005 special issue of *The Journal for Specialists in Group Work* devoted to his career.

The Board of Visitors was established in 1983, bringing together leading authorities in education, business, and culture. One member, Fred Hechinger, president of the New York Times Foundation, had published "Schoolyard Blues: The Decline of Public Education" four years earlier, calling for a national commission.[53] Hechinger's call proved prophetic when the National Commission on Excellence in Education issued *A Nation at Risk* in April 1983.

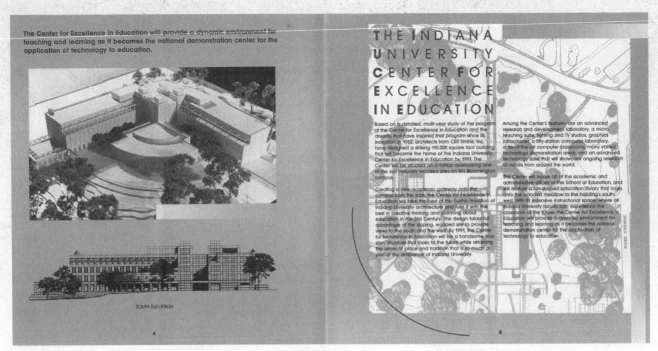

The Indiana University Center for Excellence in Education" publication (circa 1989)
showing the proposed model of the new Wendell W. Wright Education Center.

Howard Mehlinger would capitalize on the moniker of excellence when he initiated plans the same year for a Center for Excellence in Education. In September, a prospectus for such a center at Indiana University declared, "Only a Rip van Winkle could be unaware of growing public concern about the quality of schooling in America." The prospectus argued that the nation had moved "from the industrial to the information age," but "this social metamorphosis caught public schools in an institutional lag."[54] Knowing that a national showcase of educational technology and excellence was more likely to garner financial support than a new building for a school of education, Mehlinger successfully attracted funds, integrated demonstration site and school, and built the building anyway.[55]

In 1983 in a breakthrough, Robert Arnove, professor of international and comparative education, Chancellor's Professor Emeritus, took the first cohort of students to Hangzhou University in China on a program started with Mehlinger. Once again, the school led the way for the university. Also in 1983 the Department of Counseling and Educational Psychology was created by a merger of counseling and counselor education, educational inquiry methodology, educational psychology, and school psychology. The American Psychological Association accredited the counseling psychology program in 1988. The powerhouse addition of counseling psychology brought new directions and scholarly invigoration to the department but also a turning away from older centers of achievement such as school counseling.

School of Education students at Hangzhou University in China in May 1983.

One of the smartest things the school did in the 1980s was something it did not do. Several Big Ten universities (University of Michigan, Michigan State University, Ohio State University), following the "excellence"-inspired reforms of the mid-1980s, switched their undergraduate teacher education programs to the graduate level.[56] IU's School of Education did not join the crowd. Almost immediately, Big Ten schools that had made the conversion experienced budget shortfalls and saw undergraduate tuition vanish. University of Michigan downsized its education school sharply.

At IU, however, the second half of the 1980s witnessed no letup in advancements in the School of Education. In 1985 Gerald Marker, professor of secondary education (social studies), was the first director of COTEP (Coalition for Teacher Education Programs), a research and advocacy organization comprising Ball State University, Indiana State University, Purdue University, Butler University, and the University of Evansville. COTEP published recommendations for strengthening teacher education in membership schools and presented a united front for state funding.

In 1985 Roger Farr, professor of language education, created the Center for Reading and Language Studies, which he directed until 1992. Farr was a well-known developer of basal reading tests. Meanwhile, plans for a new building were percolating. On April 17, 1985, a conceptual vision of the proposed Center for Educational Excellence took shape. Tom Gregory, a professor in Curriculum and Instruction and chair of the effort, reported four basic functions of the center: innovation of ideas, research and development, demonstration of promising ideas, and dissemination of successful practices.[57]

One promise had already taken shape. In 1984 Donald Warren, who would be dean in six years, published *Pride and Promise: Schools of Excellence for All the People*, a counter-narrative to *A Nation at Risk*. Written with Mary Anne Raywid and Charles A. Tesconi, Jr., the pamphlet argued that the alarm of national risk was both overrated and understated. Schools cannot change economic conditions, the authors asserted, and teachers cannot cure the ills of society. Without agreement on the purpose of education and how schools can improve, and without reliable evidence, educational reform is meaningless, they said. Warren and colleagues cautioned that sweeping pronouncements of failure do not account for individual success. They contended that excellence cannot be mandated, equity and excellence are compatible, and schools must teach how to think and order one's affairs with respect for others. Erasure of systemic barriers is society's responsibility, they maintained, and schools cannot be expected to provide ever greater futures. Better to aim for sustainable achievement than a Shangri-la of unlimited development.

Donald Warren.

The school experienced another year of firsts in 1986. The Education Information Resource Center (ERIC), sponsored by the Institute of Education Sciences of the US Department of Education, moved part of its operation from Boulder, Colorado, to Bloomington. The Social Studies Development Center, cradle of deans Mehlinger and Terrence Mason, was awarded a contract for the social studies/social science clearinghouse. John J. Patrick, professor of education, was its first director.

Also in 1986, Martha McCarthy, education policy professor, created and directed the Consortium on Education Policy Studies with Lilly Endowment funds. The consortium became the Indiana Education Policy Center, which McCarthy led until 1992. It was folded into the current Center for Evaluation and Education Policy. In a memo to Indiana legislators and other education policymakers on April 11, 1986, McCarthy wrote that the new consortium would "provide education policymakers state of the art information on a range of policy alternatives, evaluative information, and research findings and development studies (state of the science)."[58] The consortium's steering committee included representatives from the Indiana Department of Education, school boards, the state budget agency, the Indiana State Teachers Association, House and Senate education committee chairs, the office of the governor, and the School of Education administration.

Martha McCarthy.

McCarthy's memo defined an era when stakeholders worked together and solicited expertise of the school. That era ended a decade later when, as education professor Barry Bull, successor to McCarthy, said, "the Legislature stopped talking to the Center."[59] The legislature was developing its own perspective on education such as advocating for privatization of education.

In fall 1986 the COTEP policy board issued a report, acknowledging the support of Lilly Endowment, and made 40 recommendations for improving teacher education, including forgivable loans, attracting minority students, integrating educational and liberal arts curricula, and recognizing that teaching is an art as well as a science. The report warned: "We are in the early stages of another teacher shortage....We must help our graduates feel better about having chosen teaching as a profession. The tarnished image of teachers and teaching must concern each of us, for we, too, are teachers." Drawn together by a concern over shortages and image, COTEP members pledged collective action to improve teacher education programs. "Curriculum change is a locally oriented enterprise," they asserted.[60] That conviction is not shared by many state legislatures today. Topping off 1986, AT&T gave the school $7 million to purchase AT&T equipment for the new building, approved by the trustees in 1988.

In the last three years of the 1980s, with a $700,000 grant from Lilly Endowment, Christine Bennet, professor of curriculum and instruction, founded and directed a graduate teacher education program, Teacher as Decision Maker, for middle and secondary school teachers of diverse populations. All the while, working quietly and steadily, the indispensable David Kinman directed Educational Placement and Education Student Services. Kinman possessed a personal statesmanship, vision of curriculum, mastery of licensure and certification, and unshakeable commitment to student assistance, unmatched in Indiana. He became assistant dean for education student services in 1990.

In 1987 the school was ranked number one in "Linking College of Education Productivity to Published Articles," issued by the National Association of Secondary Principals. Harmon Baldwin, superintendent of the Monroe County Community School Corporation, received the Outstanding Alumnus Award. Reading department pioneer Leo Fay created the Center for Adolescent Studies. Instructional Systems Technology ranked number one in the nation in *Performance and Instruction Journal*, March 1988. In 1989, Mehlinger and Ben Eklof, professor in the Department of History, established and codirected the Institute for Soviet Education. Ground was broken for the Center for Excellence in Education on June 15, 1989. Worldly and genial champion of adult literacy, Harbans Bhola, professor of educational leadership and policy studies, directed the Center for International Activities and Policy Study.

(*L to R*) Former IU President John W. Ryan, Governor Evan Bayh, and IU President Thomas Ehrlich at the new education building groundbreaking ceremony in 1989.

In 1990 the indefatigable Susan Eklund, professor of educational psychology and former coordinator of the school psychology program, directed the Center for Aging and Aged. Later Eklund became Byron A. Root Professor in Aging. The Office of Summer Sessions and Special Programs joined forces, reprising the role that prospective teachers played in summer school programs in the 19th century.

On July 1, 1990, Howard Mehlinger, no longer dean, became full-time director of the Center for Excellence in Education. A vehicle to transform education, the center gave birth to a building and then became part of it. Mehlinger could look back on the success of the new building with only one regret. When the IU Board of Trustees was prepared to approve funds for the building, incoming president Thomas Ehrlich won a postponement of the decision and later cut $8 million from the project. Mehlinger said, "It was the most disappointing experience of my entire career at Indiana University."[61] The school lost a wing but gained flight.

Donald Warren had taken over from Mehlinger earlier that summer as first university dean of the School of Education, a title that represented his administration of the Bloomington and IUPUI schools of education and responsibilities for education programs and faculties on IU's six other campuses. Historian of education and policy expert from the University of Maryland, Warren appointed half the faculty in his 10-year deanship. If Mehlinger's entrepreneurship gave the school a building (even if any self-respecting dean wants to be remembered for more than a building), Warren's research-oriented scholarship and critical thinking cultivated the school during an avalanche of retirements. Hiring many faculty was a chance to redefine the school not just by retirement but by the appeal to prospective faculty of world-class departments in the College of Arts and Sciences across campus. One of Warren's first acts as dean was charging the Bloomington and Indianapolis schools "to devise an action plan for creating at Indiana University teacher education programs that are first among the most exciting, cutting-edge, prophetic programs in the United States...reporting their plan back to me by March 1, 1991."[62]

Prophesy or eschatology, the era presented a millennial challenge. Technology for the new building, purchased in the late 1980s, was already outdated, and there was no money in the budget for updates. Faculty retirements over the decade raised the question: What would happen to the character of the professoriate? Rumblings were erupting in the core-campus relationship between Bloomington and Indianapolis. A new university president had cut the budget for the new building. Reading wars collapsed the umbrella of whole language and phonics. Public schools were accused of secularism. Culture battles over gay rights, abortion, and identity politics divided the population. Particularism threatened a shared sense of nationhood. Consensus on the role of education was illusory. As Donald Warren himself reflected much later, "The more we look back on *Nation At Risk*, that decade was a bubble that burst. It did not incentivize Congressional action."[63]

More than the oracular would be required to steer the ship of education; but if history was any guide, no fortune-telling was necessary to know that when the school needed leaders, the right ones appeared. Donald Warren was that leader. On March 5, 1991, his task force on teacher education issued its report, *The Future of Teacher Education at Indiana University–Bloomington*. It declared that teacher education must become a top priority; clear goals were needed; Indiana University should consider teacher education one of its highest priorities; and the teacher education program should play a central role in every unit of the school.

It was one thing for William Lowe Bryan in 1902 to say that Indiana University had been a large teacher's college. It was quite another thing at the end of the 20th century to say that IU, a modern multiversity, should make teacher education one of its highest priorities. Preparing teachers was not generally atop the agenda of major research universities.

Warren's 1990 charge and the faculty report took Indiana University to task while returning the School of Education to its roots. Could teacher education once again become a defining identity of IU, albeit under vastly changed circumstances? Could the school respond creatively to its self-imposed challenge? The stakes were high and as with any investment, especially innovation, there was risk; but the school had an agenda, and its dean was leading the way.

New dean and old school had more than teacher education to reimagine. Other horizons included a new counseling and educational psychology program, the use of appropriate technology, educational leadership and policy, multidisciplinary research, partnerships, service, student teaching, and international programs. The future as always was wide open. Old and new were off to a bold start, and courage would be needed.

# CHAPTER 5

# New Building, New Beginnings (1992–2023)

Not since the 1840s when Indiana University struggled to keep its doors open, and the state provided no money, and Hoosiers chafed at East Coast preacher presidents and professors, and a lawmaker argued against a tax for public schools saying it would lead to "extravagance and folly, law and ruin"—not for 180 years have teachers and their colleagues faced the adverse conditions they face today in a society they are trying to serve.[64]

Since 2005, obstacles for public education and for the school have included penalties for schools not meeting national standards despite structural and historic inequalities, an attempt to decertify the School of Education secondary teacher education program, an attempt to merge the school with another unit of the university, diversion of public funds to charter schools, statutory limitations on what teachers can say in classrooms or with administrators, banned books, school shootings, teacher burnout from the COVID-19 pandemic, salaries below college peers, shrinking autonomy, and a mandate to inform parents if their children want to be called by certain pronouns. Only a Rip van Winkle could be unaware of the challenges that teachers, librarians, counselors, public schools, and teacher educators confront today.

In 1937, not long after he became president of Indiana University, Herman Wells said, "Learning has blazed the way along which civilization has slowly and painfully moved forward." He called the progress of society "slow and toilsome."[65] Wells could have been talking about education today—its painful and toilsome advance. But for 100 years the Indiana University School of Education has held its head high. It has kept faith with the state's principles, enshrined in constitution and assembly, to bring education to every door, even when the door is closed. The task has not been easy, and it cannot be done alone. Some years were more productive than others, enrollments up or down, ratings ranging from top 10 to top 25 in the country, but the school has never stalled. Morale today is strong. Faculty and student hopes are high but realistic. Good work goes on.

Democracy has assigned itself no harder task than public schooling. Education is both the cause and the effect of social change, so it must lead and follow. It takes ethics and understanding to lead the crowd and be responsible to it. The School of Education has respectfully spoken truth to power while honoring fundamental values of learning and teaching, mental health, public service, scholarly research, and creative activity.

The call rings true today that brought 10 students and one teacher to Indiana Seminary in 1820.[66] As one current teacher education undergraduate from Spiceland, Indiana said, "Someone's gotta be there to lead in the next generation."[67] His high school had a graduating class of 59. He is still in touch with one of his teachers. That kind of relationship and conviction keeps students answering the call to teach, counsel, and lead.

For the same reason, it is common in the School of Education to find professors and staff at their posts for 30, 40, 50 years. Five staff—Sue Schaffer, Louise Routt, Sandy Strain, Sarah Crandall, and David Kinman—served a total of 193 years. Five faculty—Rex Stockton, Gary Ingersoll, Frank Lester, George Kuh, and Myrtle Scott—served a total of 188 years.

Despite clouds on the horizon, there is cause to celebrate, and when was public education ever cloudless? When it succeeds, however, and in a small town in Indiana with 59 students in the graduating class, it is succeeding mightily—it is because people rally to the cause of public education—not just teachers, counselors, coaches, administrators, or schools of education, but communities, volunteers, and citizens.

From his first day in office in fall 1990, Donald Warren, dean of the school, rallied his readers to "the utter importance" of education.[68] When Warren moved into the new building on Seventh Street the next year, the school's new home shone in the sun with bright limestone walls, many windows, and gleaming, white-capped towers. The new building was a physical symbol of the job of education—grounded but soaring.

New Wendell W. Wright Education Building under construction in 1992.

Faculty, staff, and students were arriving to new classrooms, laboratories, counseling clinic, auditorium, library, atrium, offices, A-V studio, departmental suites, and conference rooms, all with the latest electronic equipment. Unfazed by dazzling amenities, however, the historian in Warren knew that the world-class status of the school predated the new building and "will outlive it—if we continue to nurture" it.[69]

Nurture it, he did. He increased faculty ranks with highly qualified candidates. Reflecting later on his hiring duties, he said, "if you don't change demography, you don't change the conversation."[70] He oversaw a reform of teacher education and encouraged a critical-analytical perspective on technology for best practices. He fostered international programs and made sure the school was respected by senior administrators across campus. He raised funds and encouraged research. Soon after he arrived, he showed his true colors: He hired two dynamic faculty to a new doctoral program, even though the initial hire announcement was for one. Warren had something in him of the social gospel of William Lowe Bryan, the school's founder.

When President Bryan welcomed a conference of high school principals to Indiana University in Bloomington in 1923, the year from which the school dates its 100th birthday, he said:

> The young people are led into the schools in always larger numbers, partly by the lure of athletics and of society, partly by the legal advantages of the certificate of graduation, partly by the increasing demand of every occupation for persons of more training, and partly, we may hope, by the never-dying instinct of human beings to know more of the truth.[71]

Bryan continued: "In bidding the principals welcome to the University, I wish for you and your schools what I ardently desire for this school, that the morale of students and teachers may be so full of health that all other problems will take care of themselves."[72]

Newly constructed Wendell W. Wright Education Building in 1992.

The bright new building at Seventh Street and Rose Avenue was a new beginning for Donald Warren and a new beginning for the School of Education. It must have felt as if everything had taken care of itself. Warren said at the building's dedication in March 1993, "As each day of dedication week passed, I kept thinking that the high point had been reached, that tomorrow's events could not possibly be better. In fact, it was a week of high points."[73]

Typical of professors, not everyone was pleased with the building. Technology was anathema to some faculty. Many had to give up larger offices across campus. On the other hand, because faculty and staff had been spread across the university, they felt a new morale and community in the building—perhaps even a chance to rekindle Bryan's belief in the never-dying, human instinct to know more of the truth – not all and not just to know – but to want to know more. The hope of education is less in knowing than wanting to know.

Knowing less of the truth, however, was the danger Martha McCarthy faced in her 1991 Tracy Sonneborn Lecture. One of the nation's leading authorities on education law, McCarthy was professor of educational leadership and policy studies and founder of the Indiana Education Policy Center. In her Sonneborn address, channeling threats today, McCarthy said: "I'm concerned that as we elect boards that want to burn books and curtail expression, what actually will go up in smoke is the US Constitution, and we will be educating a generation of students who won't experience the free exchange of ideas....We can't sanitize the curriculum to the point that no group is offended....Some attitudes, such as respect for diversity, should not be compromised."[74]

Donald Warren did not compromise on quality or free exchange of ideas. He created the Dean's Advisory Council in 1994 so students could give him their opinions, and he called his audience to task at the spring dedication of the new Wendell W. Wright Education Building. With 500 guests in attendance, President Thomas Ehrlich conferring honorary degrees, and fanfare and procession in the building's atrium, Warren gave himself the historian's prerogative, invoking shoulders on which Indiana educators stand:

Dean Donald Warren speaks at the School of Education building dedication ceremony in 1993.

> We are here to celebrate a beginning. As we marvel at new surroundings, and new technology, and new capabilities, we might ponder old commitments of our forebears. Consider Nebraska Cropsey, in 1913, the fourth person—and the first woman—to receive an honorary degree from Indiana University....Indianapolis schoolteacher, assistant superintendent, developer of primary school curricula, and, as a reformer, inspired a city...she played a principal role in securing enactment of the State's compulsory education law in 1897.[75]

Warren quoted President Bryan who conferred the degree on Cropsey in 1923 and said her "obvious monument" was the schools of her city. "Led by the likes of Nebraska Cropsey, these schools were most successful when they brought up Indianapolis children 'ready to do the world's work and able also to sing,'" Warren said, quoting Bryan again.[76]

For years teaching was women's work; but on the faculty of the School of Education, it was men's. After 10 years as dean, Warren did as much to hire female faculty as any dean in the school's history.[77] Enrollment figures were singing in the early 1990s. Together, Bloomington and IUPUI schools of education were the largest teacher preparation institutions in the state. A national search was launched to hire a director of teacher education in Bloomington. Given the school's world-class technology, Warren insisted that faculty wrestle with the question of how to put it to good use. Would technology contribute to the education of critically minded citizens capable of solving problems or be frittered away on foolish memorization and isolated facts, as Emeritus Professor of Education Shirley H. Engle asked?[78] That question is alive and well in the school today.

In 1992 Barry Bull and Robert Arnove created a new PhD program in education policy studies. Bull directed the Indiana Policy Center for six years. It later merged with the current Center for Evaluation and Education Policy.

Robert Arnove.

An immediate opportunity to test technology's best practices was distance education. In summer 1993, the school offered its first distance education class via two new A-V studios in education buildings in Bloomington and Indianapolis. Compressed video was installed on each campus, allowing an A-V signal to travel over telephone lines. The interactive benefit, plus the concurrent understanding of how to deploy the technology, were compound advantages. In what today seems like a primitive ancestor of the video communication platform Zoom, the A-V setup was designed to take education to every door instead of students having to come to campus. The technologies were cutting edge for their day.

Then-modern technology was not yet double-edged. Presciently in 1994 Kris Bosworth, director of the school's Center for Adolescent Studies, could have had distracted adolescents in mind when she began two projects to help teens reach their potential. In one study, Bosworth found that adolescents have little ability for long-range planning. She urged schools and communities to give them practice establishing long-range goals and developing relationships with adults who care about their academic future. In another study, funded by the National Centers for Disease Control and Prevention, Bosworth created a program to help teenagers resolve conflicts nonviolently.

In 1994, Christine Bennett, professor of curriculum and instruction, directed a new Research Institute on Teacher Education to study alternative education programs. The project fostered multidisciplinary and collaborative research among faculty and students in the School of Education, the College of Arts and Sciences, and public schools. If change is the name of education, the question for reforms was how to institutionalize change.

In 1995 Robert Arnove, professor of leadership and policy studies, received the John W. Ryan Award for Distinguished Contributions to International Programs and Studies, Indiana University's highest recognition for international achievement. In 1996 the Armstrong Teacher Educator award and chair were established, both made possible through the Martha Lea and Bill Armstrong Fund in Teacher Education by a gift from Cook Group Companies of Bloomington. (When Bill Cook died in 2011, Hoosier rock musician John Mellencamp made a major contribution to the Armstrong Fund in Cook's name.)

The Armstrong Teacher Educator Award recognizes outstanding teachers in Indiana and brings them to Bloomington to interact with students and faculty. One Armstrong teacher (2010–2011) from a school in Indianapolis said she was "a rock star" in her school. When she came to Bloomington to speak to students, she said, "there were 300 of them and they listened to me!"[79]

Consummate listener, mentor, and pioneering advocate of service learning was the widely respected Thomas Froehle, professor of counseling psychology. Froehle was elected vice president in 1996 of the American Education Research Association (Division E: Counseling and Human Development). Able to work with a wide range of students' interests, giving mentees maximum freedom with minimum supervision, Froehle brought together

Donald Warren speaks at the outside teaching area dedication at the IU School of Education in 1994.

Bloomington community stakeholders, academic programs, and campus organizations for mutually beneficial educational projects. He worked to establish a center for service learning, often saying that the people in need of service were best served by serving others.

Whether incorporating service learning or research, curriculum is always being rewritten, best done at the local level. Some kind of teacher education reform at Indiana University is as dependable as daffodils in spring, but in the late 1990s it had been two decades since the School of Education had enacted as sweeping a reform as it did in response to Donald Warren's charge. His Bloomington task force had called for teacher education to be *primus inter pares* in the school, a top priority in the university, and central to every school department. After a national search, the man chosen to lead the reform was Landon E. Beyer, a 48-year-old educational theorist. Beyer was appointed in 1994, first as director, then as associate dean of teacher education. A lanky pilgrim of equality who enjoyed a good laugh, Lanny Beyer was author of eight books on democracy, education, and curriculum theory and a graduate of the University of Wisconsin. He was already a prolific author and leading advocate of social justice through education when he came to Bloomington.

Early in 1997 Beyer invited school faculty in all departments to share visions of teacher education. Conversations began in large groups. A conceptual framework for reform emerged with six principles: community; critical reflection; intellectual, personal, and professional growth; meaningful experience; knowledge and multiple forms of understanding; and personalized learning. Large, multidisciplinary groups broke into smaller program areas in elementary, middle, secondary, and special education. Over the following year, reformers met in the school and each other's homes to prepare final proposals.

One such proposal was Democracy, Diversity, and Social Justice, an elementary teacher education program. Faculty and graduate student members of the working group came from language education, social studies, policy studies, elementary education, counseling and educational psychology, special education, anthropology of education, math education, comparative education, student advising, student teaching, graduate programs, and an elementary school in the Bloomington community.

The program was short-lived, but lessons learned were lasting. Dwindling state appropriations had increased enrollment pressures, and the program had a small enrollment despite attempts to attract students. Although the program was discontinued, the benefits of interdisciplinary faculty collaboration bore fruit when a new teacher education course created by the counseling department set enrollment records.

"Communication in the Classroom (G203)," a three-credit course offered by the Department of Counseling and Educational Psychology, was a happy outcome of a shortened reform. The course applied counseling techniques and attitudes to teaching. Many meetings between teacher and counselor education faculty led to endorsement of the course by teacher education programs. Required today by all programs, the course was an instant success when it launched in 1997.

G203 filled a need and appealed to a desire in both teacher education and counseling and educational psychology. The course allowed counseling doctoral students to serve as associate instructors under faculty supervision. The large number of sections gave master's students a chance to teach as well. All instructors earned a stipend and fee remission. It was a win-win situation: Teacher education students had no other classes in which they learned what G203 taught—classroom management, positive climate, and facilitative communication. Graduate students in counseling had few opportunities to teach. The course permitted the School of Education to capture credit that had been going to the College of Arts and Sciences to satisfy licensure requirements for coursework in communication, now better designed and delivered in the school.

Counseling and educational psychology maintained an impact on teacher education via the course. G203 students learned positive attitudes such as empathy, genuineness, and respect, and interpersonal practices of self-disclosure, confrontation, and verbal feedback. The course curriculum helped preservice teachers shape cooperative classrooms rich in expression, reflective listening, self-motivated learning, and group problem solving in a psychologically healthy educational setting.

Meanwhile, two older teacher education programs were also thriving. Community of Teachers (COT) started soon after the new building opened. Teacher as Decision Maker, a graduate-level program, had been operating since 1988. COT was the brainchild of Tom Gregory and Kris Bosworth. Gregory was a scholar of small and alternative schools; Bosworth, an expert on adolescence. Both were professors in curriculum and instruction. The decision-maker program was started by Christine Bennett in curriculum and instruction with funding from Lilly Endowment. Bennett's initiative trained people who had earned the baccalaureate degree or advanced degrees in other fields but wished to change careers.

COT attracted Susan Klein, special education professor. Klein called COT "a secondary multidisciplinary program, including future special education teachers, that got away from the idea of a program as a sequence of courses."[80] Students picked a seminar taught by faculty that became a place to share what was happening in their student teaching. Students took control of their education by seeking and finding a mentor teacher, helping to recruit new members to the program, and designing instructional portions of the seminar. COT "emphasizes empowerment of teachers," Klein said, "to become the teachers they want to be. The program enacts a sense of community, social responsibility, self-assessment, modeling of best practices, authentic performance and evaluation, collaboration between faculty and students, and long-term faculty–student relationships."[81]

The special character of COT came from Gregory's experience in a small alternative high school in Colorado in 1981 where he spent a sabbatical year. "It was a 1-person, 1-vote school, run by students," he said. "Everybody who had a stake in the school had a say in the school."[82] Reflecting on his experience at the open school in Colorado, Gregory wrote a poignant story of a high school boy named Toby May who was killed in an automobile accident.[83] Without mentioning a word about pedagogy, Gregory described Mountain Open High School in terms of the emotional bonds between students and of students who came together around their friend's death. May, a charismatic and free-wheeling spirit, had said that when he died he wanted his friends to decorate his coffin. His parents invited his friends to draw on the casket before his funeral. As friends arrived to mourn but mostly celebrate their quirky friend and his unconditional embrace of life, their antics and emotions expressed the love and community that Mountain Open High School taught. That kind of education is not preparation for life, it is life.

The experience of Toby May and an open high school in Colorado was also a lesson for Tom Gregory. From his 1970s innovative introduction to teaching to his 1980 experience at Mountain Open High School, Gregory has sought to create lively and meaningful environments for would-be teachers and mentors to grow emotionally, thoughtfully, quirkily, and communally.

In his car coming back to Indiana from Colorado in 1981, the 43-year-old Gregory had a 22-hour drive "and nothing to think about but how to build a teacher education program to prepare teachers for an open school." The idea took time and space to percolate. "We had just gone into the new building," he said, "and Kris Bosworth was hanging out in the hallway one day and said, 'We ought to start a teacher education program.'" I thought, 'I can do that as badly as anyone.'"

Mountain Open High School was rekindled. Bosworth and he began meeting. "We planned for undergraduate and master's students who wanted a different kind of experience," he said. "We had doctoral students from five continents. Kris and I were the only faculty members, and then Susan Klein came along. Rock Bonchek from Harmony School was part of it, too." [84]

To design the program, Gregory drew on his introductory course from 20 years ago. As well, many of his ideas for COT were illustrated, often literally, in his experimental and self-guided 1974 text, *Teaching Is*, written with Merrill Harmon. Gregory said, "I was thought of as a young Turk then. Lee Ehman was one."[85]

Hobbled by health woes today that "cost me a lost year,"[86] the young Turk is now a gray eminence on a different ride across new country. He still lives and laughs on the frontiers of educational innovation and emotional community, animated by Toby May, good conversation, and the necessity of teacher self-knowledge and self-determination, still wondering, "What would a good teacher education program look like?"

For the most part, the 1990s closed on a high note. George Kuh, professor of educational leadership and policy studies, who became a giant in the field of college student engagement and quality of higher education, conceived the National Survey of Student Engagement as a new approach to gathering information about collegiate institutional quality. The idea was piloted in 1999 with funding from the Pew Charitable Trusts and became an institution of its own.

In 1997 Jerome Harste, professor of language education; Christine Leland at IUPUI; and a group of public school teachers created a new public school in Indianapolis, the Center for Inquiry. It enrolled 150 students to explore multiple ways-of-knowing and inquiry-based learning in a multi-age, holistic setting. Today there are four such schools in Indianapolis, and a high school on the drawing board.

The School of Education has always been good about hiring people with practical experience and giving them authority for real problems. A good example was C. Frederick Risinger. A veteran teacher and administrator in public schools, Risinger was the perfect fit to advance career-long professional growth in educators and advise deans and faculty. Over the years, the school relied heavily on him. Among his many appointments, he was coordinator for school social studies (1973–1988) and director of professional development, school services, and summer sessions in 1997. Fred Risinger's experience and common sense helped bring the hallways of actual schools to the ivory tower.

Innovations continued. In 1998 the Barbara B. Jacobs Chair in Education and Technology was established. Another first was the Center for Research on Learning and Technology, started in 1999 and operating today. The center studies novel connections and environments of technology and learning, including robotics, the internet, mobile phones, and video games. One wonders what the far-sighted architects of the post-World War II A-V Center, using lantern slides, overhead transparencies, and closed-circuit TV, would think of today's technology; or what future architects of technique will think of ours.

In 1999 Indiana University established the Center for Education and Society to encourage social-science-based research on education around important questions of educational policy and practice. The Center provided a framework for faculty and graduate students in education and sociology to collaborate on research and field work. In spring 1999 the IU Center for Postsecondary Research in the School of Education partnered with the IU Center for Survey Research to administer George Kuh's National Survey of Student Engagement for the first time, trying it out at 12 institutions. Since then, about 1,400 institutions and two million students in the US and Canada have participated.

Also in 1999, Edward McClellan published *Moral Education in America: Schools and the Shaping of Character from Colonial Times to the Present* with Teachers College Press. Professor of history of education, twice editor of *History of Education Quarterly*, and acting editor of the *Journal of American History*, McClellan was a national leader of scholarly associations, twice chair of the Department of Educational Leadership and Policy Studies, and executive associate dean of the school.

One disappointment at the end of the decade foretold a break in valuable communication between the School of Education and the Indiana legislature. Barry Bull, executive associate dean under Donald Warren, referring to the Indiana Center for Evaluation that he directed, said that "in the late 1990s the Legislature stopped talking to us. They had their own perspective on education, such as the privatization of education."[87] Gone were the days when Martha McCarthy brought together legislators, the governor's office, School of Education leaders, teachers' union officials, school boards, and the State Budget Agency to discuss educational policy. Financially, if not politically, things were on track: From 1990 to 1998 the school's endowment grew from nearly $2 million to more than $14.7 million.

Donald Warren hosted IU's International Alumni Conference and Reunion in Chiang Mai, Thailand in summer 2000. Two hundred former students attended. School of Education alumni were the largest group. In Europe that summer, John Patrick, professor of social studies, was working in war-weary Bosnia-Herzegovina, helping preservice teachers teach democratic principles.

Gerardo Gonzalez.

In fall 2000 the school welcomed Gerardo Gonzalez as university dean. Surviving a revolution in his homeland, the Cuban American and his family left Castro's Cuba when Gonzalez was a child. His father brought his family to the United States with next to no money in his pocket. The young Gonzalez soon discovered the salvation of public education. He never forgot the ladder that education offered him. He made sure everyone appreciated the leg up offered to them. Nor did he forget to dance. Gonzalez rarely missed the chance to take the dance floor at school parties and always hired the best of bands. In speeches or commentaries the "dancing dean" refused to keep his music in him, sharing the inspiration of education.

Throughout his 15-year tenure (second longest serving dean in school history), Gonzalez was an articulate ambassador. At the legislature he was often "the face of opposition," beginning in 2010.[88] He wrote letters to the editor, spoke publicly, and published articles. He defended teachers and teacher educators against shortsighted attacks from within the house of government. Given the delicate relationship between the state university and the state of Indiana, it would have been easy to remain silent, but he spoke truth to power.

Beginning in 2001, he confronted No Child Left Behind (NCLB), the national policy that penalized schools for not meeting NCLB standards. Poor and underperforming schools deserved reward, not punishment. He fought the so-called reform efforts of Indiana Superintendent of Public Instruction Tony Bennett's Rules for Educator Preparation and Accountability (REPA).[89] The rules revised educator licensing structure and tried to decertify the school's secondary program. Falsely attacked for the slim number of history courses in the school's secondary curriculum, Gonzalez told the legislature that not only did secondary education students take plenty of history and social studies courses, but they took more courses than history majors in the College of Arts and Sciences.[90] Despite smears on public education from those supposed to protect it, school faculty in 2000 received $15 million in grants and contracts.[91]

Charged by its Policy Council in 2000, the school drafted a long-range strategic plan, initiated by Gonzalez in 2002. The plan called for the school to meet five goals: continue its commitment to strong preservice teacher education; strengthen partnerships with prekindergarten through 12th-grade schools and communities; enhance and expand the school's research and other scholarly and creative activities while strengthening the quality of graduate programs; provide leadership in the appropriate use of technologies to enhance teaching and learning experiences; and promote diversity. Each goal was accompanied by related tasks. Goals and tasks were not prioritized.[92]

One of Gerardo Gonzalez's first acts in office was to distribute $200,000 he had negotiated with Bloomington Chancellor and Executive Vice President Kenneth Gros Louis to create online courses. He tapped school reserves to give laptop computers to faculty who proposed projects that aligned with strategic goals. He won authorization to initiate the direct-admit program that enrolled high-achieving secondary students directly into the school. He improved the quality and quantity of scholarships, targeted minority hires of faculty, and established the Center for Teaching and Learning and the Global and International Engagement office.

In addition to opposing REPA, Gonzalez warned publicly that charter schools lacked rigorous documentation of performance. He kept cause with public education as it faced dissolution by "improvement." He never wavered in his conviction that the school or its graduates, despite political hostility, would adapt and succeed. His 2005 message is relevant today:

> It cannot be denied that the school choice movement is changing America's educational landscape. Is it changing it for the better? That has yet to be determined....To some, school choice is the silver bullet....There are also those who believe the school choice movement is part of a larger effort to bring about the demise of public education....Although no one can foresee how current school reform trends will unfold in the coming years, we do know

that our faculty will be actively shaping the future of education through their teaching, research, and service. And our students will be well-prepared to meet whatever professional challenges they encounter.[93]

From 2000 to 2003 Jack Cummings served as executive associate dean of the school, and again from 2010 to 2011. A school psychologist, Cummings had been chair of Counseling and Educational Psychology. His command of detail, manifest integrity, and familiarity with the school provided critical in-house teamwork when the dean was fighting battles abroad. The reflective demeanor of the second-in-command complemented Gonzalez's impassioned engagement. Cummings was a pioneering researcher of the practice of school psychology in rural settings before chairing his department. He led national invitational conferences on the future of school psychology. If the School of Education had deans at the right moment, it also had timely executive associate deans.

The activist special education professor Ellen Brantlinger in 2003 won a national award for her study of the disadvantages accruing to lower income students when higher income parents use cultural capital to advantage their children. Her *Classes Divided: How the Middle Class Negotiates and Rationalizes Advantage* was one of four Outstanding Books chosen by the American Educational Research Association Division B (Curriculum and Curriculum Studies), demonstrating the effects of class structure on schooling. "Social class is an important determinant of status and social interactions," she said in an interview. "Once children are marked not only by social class status, but also by stigmatizing labels and dumbed-down placements, their personal identity is affected. Their sense of self further impairs their cognitive development."[94]

Rex Stockton in Botswana.

In 2004 Rex Stockton, professor of counseling psychology, started a 20-year project in Botswana helping African professionals work with HIV-AIDS patients. Many of Stockton's graduate students accompanied him during the project. He became Chancellor's Professor the same year. Also that year, Jonathan Plucker in counseling and educational psychology succeeded Edward St. John as director of the Indiana Education Policy Center. St. John had directed the policy center since 1997. He is now emeritus professor of education, University of Michigan, where he was the Algo D. Henderson Collegiate Professor of Education. Plucker was associate professor in the school at the time. He is now the Julian C. Stanley Endowed Professor of Talent Development at Johns Hopkins University.

The school in 2004 announced a new initiative to help the state offer continuous education from prekindergarten through high school. With funding from Lilly Endowment and coleadership in the Monroe County school system, Community Alliances to Promote Education Project set up family resource centers in 11 townships of Monroe County to provide families with educational, social, health, and psychological services.

The Center for Evaluation and Education Policy (CEEP) launched in 2004. It was a merger of the Indiana Center for Evaluation and the Indiana Education Policy Center. Jonathan Plucker, its founding director, served as director from 2003 to 2012. Today CEEP takes the work of faculty to, and engages with, appropriate audiences (schools, government, media, foundations) to improve education and educational policy. The Center conducts evaluations for clients.

The year 2004 was a busy one. Former chair of the Department of Educational Psychology and Associate Dean of the Faculties Susan Eklund cofounded the Emeriti House on Atwater Avenue in Bloomington with Vice Chancellor for Academic Affairs and Dean of the Faculties Moya Andrews. The Emeriti House was the culmination of Eklund's longtime study of gerontology. It is a popular venue for socializing, art exhibits, lectures, workshops, and special projects and events for retired faculty and librarians.

In 2005 Tom Duffy, professor of learning sciences, instructional systems technology, and cognitive science, was the first Barbara B. Jacobs Chair of Education and Technology. In 2006 Anastasia Morrone, executive director of the Center for Teaching and Learning and associate professor in the School of Education at IUPUI, became associate dean for teaching and learning information technologies within the university's Information Technology Services. In 2020 Morrone became the first woman to serve as dean of the school. It took 100 years for a woman to be dean, but whoever accused history of being on time?

Terrence Mason, who directed the IU Center for Social Studies and International Education, began working in 2006 with colleague Mitzi Lewison, associate professor of language education, on the Afghanistan Higher Education Project. The effort was part of a US consortium that received a $38 million grant to restore and improve the educational system in Afghanistan. That same year professor of educational leadership and policy studies and East Asian studies, Heidi Ross, renowned scholar of Chinese education and schooling, directed Indiana University's East Asian Studies Center. The School of Education was again leading the university in bold international programs at crucial times in novel ways.

Mitzi Lewison with graduating student in Kabul, Afghanistan.

In 2007 the school's graduate programs ranked 17th in *US News & World Report*.[95] The Center for Research and P–16 Collaboration, begun in 2006, directed by Cathy Brown, a math educator, partnered with the New Technology Foundation. The partnership provided training in project-based learning to school districts adopting the New Technology High School model. Also in 2007 the School of Education at IUPUI enhanced a longtime IU relationship with Kenya. The IU School of Medicine had operated health clinics throughout Kenya since 1989, focusing on the AIDS pandemic. Khaula Murtadha, executive associative dean of the School of Education at IUPUI, was a key coordinator. The collaboration strengthened universal education and promoted healthy lifestyles.

Approved in 2009 by the Indiana Commission for Higher Education, a new inquiry methodology PhD program in the Department of Counseling and Educational Psychology began enrolling students for fall. The same year, the Tandem Certification of Indiana Teachers partnership, and the Interdisciplinary Collaborative Program, in conjunction with the Department of Literacy, Culture, and Language Education, trained 200 teachers in Indiana in English as a second language. In 2010 there were 40 million foreign-born people living in the United States—13% of the population—the largest immigrant total in the nation's history.[96]

Storm clouds were brewing on the horizon. Enacted in 2010, REPA, under Tony Bennett's Department of Education, unleashed systematic reforms. Gerardo Gonzalez would spend the rest of his administration defending public education and the school against political attacks in the name of reform.

In 2011 the Department of Instructional Systems Technology made history. The Indiana Commission for Higher Education approved a new EdD degree in IST delivered entirely through distance education technology. The new program was the first all-online doctorate at Indiana University. Ted Frick, chair and professor of instructional systems technology, created the program, which offered the same content as the in-person design but allowed more opportunities for working professionals and others to earn the degree.

In May 2012, the Indiana Commission for Higher Education approved a new urban education studies PhD to be offered by the School of Education on the IUPUI campus in fall 2012, the first doctoral degree education program conducted entirely on the IUPUI campus.

Julian Bond, civil rights activist and former NAACP president, and Dean Gonzalez opened the INSPIRE Living-Learning Center in 2014, housed in an IU residence hall adjacent to the education building.

Civil rights leader Julian Bond speaks at the INSPIRE Living Learning Center dedication ceremony.

The exciting new opportunity for teacher education undergraduates to study and socialize together offered self-government, seminars, professional development, and service learning experiences. INSPIRE is an enthusiastic success today.

Ever the avatar of public education, Gonzalez warned in 2014 that school reform was pushing potential teachers away from the profession. He wrote:

> In Indiana, enrollment in teacher education programs has decreased by more than 30 percent over the last decade, and the rate of decrease recently has accelerated. Indiana is not unique in experiencing a drop in teacher education enrollment fueled by disinvestment in public education and contentious public policies that discourage talented students from going into teaching as well as encourage experienced teachers to leave the field. It is happening nationwide. Education reform in Indiana needs a conversation not confrontation. That conversation should start with an honest assessment of the impact of reform efforts to date.

At the same time, Indiana has implemented numerous ill-informed policies that discourage teachers from pursuing higher levels of education, promote merit pay based largely on unreliable test-based evaluation methods, lower standards for teacher licensure, and generally promote de-professionalization of teaching.[97]

Poorly informed reforms were not only an external threat. In 2015 IU President Michael McRobbie convened "a Blue Ribbon committee of education thought-leaders and practitioners to assess the structure and future direction of the university's education programs."[98] The Blue Ribbon committee was authorized at a time when McRobbie was merging and consolidating units of the university, including the School of Library and Information Science, School of Journalism, and Department of Communication and Culture. Many feared the same fate for the School of Education. Its temporary decline in enrollments was cited by the university administration as additional justification for wholesale reassessment of the school.

Terrence Mason.

Terrence Mason, who succeeded Gonzalez in 2015, referred to the Blue Ribbon committee in an e-mail to school faculty and staff on December 10, 2015: "Many of you may be wondering about the results of the Blue Ribbon Review Committee. The Committee concluded that the core-campus issue [separation of the two schools into independent schools] superseded all other issues and therefore made it difficult to offer other recommendations. As a result, the Committee's report will be withheld until the core-campus issue is resolved."[99]

The core-campus issue was resolved in 2017, but the report was never released. School of Education observers concluded the ribbon was cut because an interim report had been positive, chilling hopes for a merger. The Blue Ribbon Committee vanished as quickly as it had begun. The committee was no longer a committee, but the school remained a school.

In August 2017 the Indiana University Board of Trustees endorsed a recommendation to separate the schools of education in Bloomington and Indianapolis. From 2015 through 2018, the School of Education was a whirlwind of change—three deans in three years, almost merged, and unmerged. The Blue Ribbon committee formed in March 2015; Gonzalez returned to the faculty; Mason was appointed interim dean in July 2015 and Dean in August 2016; the core campus was dissolved in August 2017; Mason returned to the faculty, and Lemuel Watson became dean in 2018. The whirlwind quieted to a gentle breeze as two deans would step down in six more years.

Dissolution of the core campus coincided with the search for a dean. The transition from Gerardo Gonzalez in 2015 was lengthened by a year. Henry Lester Smith's 30-year tenure was a thing of the past, but the school was well prepared. When Terrence Mason became interim dean in 2015, the School of Education was in good hands again, fortunate for the right person at the right time.

Of unassailable character, genial demeanor, and strategic mind, Mason had broad and deep experience of pedagogical and global inflection points of the school. He had been a member of teacher education reform in the 1990s and director of the Center for Social Studies and International Education (formerly, Social Studies Development Center) in the 2000s. A proven problem solver, he inspired instant respect. Mason had conducted international missions for the school as professor and director. He helped build civic capacity in the Balkans and central Asia. His assignments required astute thinking, and he was able to win successful cooperation of diverse local communities in charged political environments.

Characterized by "the soul of an artist and the tact of a diplomat,"[100] Mason would need the skill of a UN ambassador to bring about a successful separation of the contentious constituencies of the IUPUI and Bloomington schools of education—a marriage without much romance. Mason not only faced a break-up but the need to achieve a functional settlement for future cooperation. IUPUI versus Bloomington proved no match after the Balkans.

"Following a long and arduous approval process," Mason said, "an agreement was reached in 2017 for each school to operate independently. As dean, I had to engage in a great deal of 'shuttle diplomacy' between Bloomington and Indianapolis to get both sides to endorse the idea. I endured many very tense meetings... but in the end the faculty on both campuses voted in favor of the change by an overwhelming majority."[101]

Termination of the core campus, which had existed since President John Ryan, was the first separation of its scale in school history. Ryan's motivation for the marriage, to shore up teacher accreditation in Indianapolis, was no longer an issue. Thanks in large part to the skillful diplomacy of Terrence Mason, the agreement enabled each school to concentrate on historic and emerging strengths to meet educational needs of the state and nation.

Another milestone in fall 2016 was the school's inaugural Elder Watson Diggs "The Dreamer" Award. Diggs (1883–1947) was the first African American to graduate from the School of Education. In honor of his legacy and graduation centennial, the school recognized three IU students with the award, and it is still being given.

Estefani Alcaraz Quevedo, Janai Weeks and Ramir Williams, first recipients of the Elder Watson Diggs "Dreamer" Award presented at the Balfour Scholars Program in the IU School of Education.

In Spring 2018 the university opened its search for a school dean. The following fall, Lemuel Watson was appointed dean, telling readers of *Chalkboard* he was "excited to be your 12th dean of the School of Education and to be a part of this exciting time in our history! We are charged to 'Re-imagine education' by IU's Grand Challenge Initiative. I know without a doubt we will succeed in our quest to continue to accomplish the unimaginable."[102] The unimaginable happened sooner than expected. Within two years, the school was looking for another dean. Watson became Indiana University associate vice president for diversity, equity, and multicultural affairs in 2020.

Under Watson's leadership, the school concluded its strategic planning and initiated diversity and inclusion programs. In October 2020, Watson and Zhu XuDong, dean of the Faculty of Education at Beijing Normal University, signed a memorandum of intent for collaboration. The School of Education ranked among the best education graduate schools in *U.S. News & World Report* and boasted eight specialty programs in the top 20.

Lemuel Watson.

Celebrating 50 years of service in 2020 was Global Gateway for Teachers, started by James Mahan when the initiative was called the Professional Year Teacher Training Program.

50th Anniversary celebration for Global Gateway for Teachers held in 2022. From left to right: David Dimmett (Executive Vice President and Chief Impact Officer, Project Lead the Way); Dawn M. Whitehead (Vice President of the Office of Global Citizenship for Campus Community, and Careers at the American Association of Colleges and Universities); Laura Stachowski (Director, Global Gateway for Teachers); James M. Mahan (Professor Emeritus, Global Gateway for Teachers Founder); Pam Fischer (Retired English Teacher); Kathleen Sideli (IU Associate Vice President for Overseas Study).

Also marking the half-century point was the Center for Human Growth in the Department of Counseling and Educational Psychology. The Center was honored in 2017 with the O'Bannon Institute for Community Service Community Partner Award, offering an effective, reliable, and affordable option for clients otherwise unable to afford counseling, according to Rex Stockton, its longtime *paterfamilias*.

It would require more than a *paterfamilias* to survive the *annus horribilis* on the horizon. In March 2020, spring break was extended, the university moved online, and the world awoke to a new coronavirus disease, soon known as COVID-19. Dislocations and loss of life caused by the virus rivaled anything the university had ever seen. Effects are still being felt, even as the US government announced on May 11, 2023, three years after the university temporarily shut its doors, that the COVID-19 Public Health Emergency was over.

In spring 2020 students and faculty transitioned to online classes. Laboratory research and other in-person activities were truncated or canceled. The social toll was extreme, particularly for first-year students whose first year was cut short and whose next year was virtual. One undergraduate who graduated in 2023 said she felt like a sophomore.[103] The university and school responded heroically, but some things were gone for good, and others changed forever. The mass use of technology to teach and meet saved the university from academic disaster and transformed the educational landscape. Meanwhile, aftershocks of the pandemic continue to impact lives, social behavior, and the international economy.

COVID-19 was on the mind of Provost Lauren Robel when she named Anastasia Morrone in 2020 as interim dean of the School of Education. The selection of Stacy Morrone was another example of the right person at the right time. At the announcement of the appointment Robel said:

Anastasia Morrone.

Stacy is the ideal person to lead the School of Education during a period when technology is more critical than ever in creating teaching and learning environments to keep students and instructors engaged and connected. Her deep relationships across the university, her commitment to excellence, and her tireless work made it possible for IU to pivot to remote instruction with integrity. She is a national leader in the use of learning technologies, and I am confident she will lead the School of Education with extraordinary skill and dedication to the school's mission.[104]

For her part, Morrone said, "I am honored and excited to have the opportunity to serve the School of Education in the role of interim dean. My entire career—as a scholar and serving in administration—has been focused on excellence in teaching and learning, and the ways in which technology helps us achieve our goals and engage with our students and colleagues, and to pursue the school's longstanding and ongoing commitment to excellence and innovation in teaching, research and service, and commitment to diversity, equity, and inclusion."[105]

Before becoming interim dean, Morrone was associate vice president of learning technologies in the Office of the Vice President for Information Technology, and professor of educational psychology at the IU Bloomington and IUPUI schools of education. The core campus dissolved, but from its solution came Stacy Morrone, whom the Bloomington campus embraced. Just as Howard Mehlinger never wanted to be remembered as the dean who built a building, Stacy Morrone was more than the first woman dean of the School of Education.

She became dean in 2021. In a review of her first year, Morrone cited advancements in the school. The traditional *Chalkboard* was renamed *Alumni Magazine* to reflect the update on chalk by keyboard. Trailing an economic downturn from COVID-19, the school was still able to move forward. "Despite a hiring freeze," Morrone said, "we were given permission to post critical new positions this fall, and we have successfully filled all of them with outstanding candidates."[106] Six new online certificates, a marketing campaign for undergraduate programs, and renovations inside the education building were also underway. In the spirit of Gerardo Gonzalez during the difficult days of so-called reforms, Morrone expressed her pride in the school's ability to bring its best to the challenges of COVID-19, "I am so proud of our School of Education community. Our faculty, staff and students have demonstrated the best in the human spirit to serve, adapt and accommodate while caring for others."[107]

Morrone's report on 2022 in the *Alumni Magazine* of spring 2023 featured the 50th anniversary of the world-class, worldwide Global Gateways for Teachers, and a new online certificate in academic advising. Also noted were a renovated and sparkling tech-rich education library made possible by school donors, a redesigned café, a newly furnished Office of Undergraduate and Teacher Education, and the start of a refurbished Center for Human Growth to serve children as well as adults. Celebrating the 30th anniversary of the "new" Wendell W. Wright Education Building in August 2022 meant improvements in comfort and efficiency to refresh a stately structure beginning to show its age.

Newly renovated education library.

Children participate in a lesson in the newly renovated education library.

Stacy Morrone agreed to extend her term of office by one year. With skill, grace, and determination, she brought education back from a viral cliff to a vital in-person community. A colleague of Morrone's who left the school to accept the Susan S. Engeleiter Chair in Education Law, Policy, and Practice at the University of Wisconsin, and who knows something about equity and leadership, said of Morrone, "She has been fair-minded."[108]

A semester before the COVID-19 pandemic, in fall 2019, the school sponsored the Robert L. Gibson Centennial Symposium, honoring the 100th birthday of the former chairman and professor of counseling and guidance (now Counseling and Educational Psychology). Gibson died in 2015. Organizers said the symposium was the first faculty centennial in school history. Gibson's colleagues, collaborators, and students gathered for two days in Bloomington, some coming from Scotland and Bermuda. Chaired by Marianne Mitchell, emerita professor of education and Gibson's longtime coauthor and friend, the event began with a keynote address that invoked Gibson's timely ethos.

The keynote speaker, a student of Gibson's in 1980, said of the man: "If democracy is to remain a system of government of people, by people, and for people, education must guide people toward democracy. The problem is that we govern ourselves. Democracy is a system of self-government. To survive, let alone thrive, we must protect ourselves from ourselves. Bob Gibson was utterly convinced that the best way to learn to govern ourselves is education."[109]

This history of the School of Education now approaches the present, a moving target. Life is lived forward but understood backward. A look around, if not quite backward, must suffice for understanding.

Centers are busy with research and engagements. Faculty teach and publish. Enrollments are strong. Recent graduates have taken jobs as teachers, counselors, and policy leaders. A socially and architecturally renewed educational community thrives inside the Wendell W. Wright Education Building. The school celebrated its 100th birthday on March 24, 2023.

Panel discussion featuring current and former deans at the 30th-anniversary dedication of the Wendell W. Wright Education Building in 2023.

Terrence Mason, Howard Mehlinger (partially obstructed), Anastasia Morrone, IU Provost Rahul Shrivastav, and Gerardo Gonzalez cut a cake at the 100th-anniversary celebration for the Wendell W. Wright Education Building.

In the atrium of the building, Stacy Morrone introduced Pamela Whitten, the first woman president of Indiana University, who gave greetings. Awards were bestowed, awardees spoke, and more speakers were still to speak. The last speech was cut short because, although education stands on the shoulders of giants, it stood that day in the shadow of a birthday cake. History will little note nor long remember what was said there, but those in attendance will not forget what they ate there. University Provost and Executive Vice President Rahul Shrivastav, with help from Deans Emeriti Howard Mehlinger and Terry Mason and Dean Stacy Morrone, cut the cake.

Birthday attendees toured a renovated education library, formally opened later to smiles and scholars. Updating included well-lit meeting rooms equipped with the latest technology, new shelves, new meeting rooms, and an open atmosphere. A spacious, glassed-in observation/simulation room for teaching reading glowed like a first-year teacher. Cubicles, communal spaces, and comfortable furniture sat alongside curved windows opening onto dell and woods. Low bookshelves allowed a clear view of Kinsey Hollow and the woodland classroom donated by Barbara Tymitz-Wolf, professor of special education, in memory of her husband Robert L. Wolf in the Department of Counseling and Educational Psychology.

The Global Gateway for Teachers continues to win awards, most recently the 2023 John W. Ryan Award for Distinguished International Programs and Studies, given to its director. Global Gateway sends student teachers to 21 countries, the Navajo Nation, and an urban program in Chicago. The program has won awards from the Institute of International Education, the Goldman Sachs Foundation, the American Association of Colleges of Teacher Education, and the School of Education for Outstanding International Engagement.

The Department of Instructional Systems Technology has been renamed the Department of Learning, Design, and Adult Education. It features nine residential and online degree programs. Learning sciences joined IST in fall of 2022, prompting the name change, although their programs have not merged. Robotics, applications of artificial intelligence, wearable technology, uses of computational thinking, STEM-inspired courses, and open resources are bright spots on the horizon of the reinvigorated department.

The Department of Counseling and Educational Psychology offers a new undergraduate major in counseling and student services, an undergraduate minor in counseling, an undergraduate minor in child and adolescent mental health, and a master's program. It has a new addictions track for its counseling master's program and a new name for its inquiry program (Qualitative and Quantitative Research Methodology). The department has already developed three online graduate certificates in the inquiry program. Its doctoral minor program in sport and performance psychology boasts curricular and clinical preparation. Department faculty teach and publish in the areas of positive psychology, addictions, autism, and qualitative and quantitative methodologies, to name a few. The newly appointed Center for Human Growth welcomes clients, trains counselors, provides supervision, and facilitates research.

The Department of Educational Leadership and Policy Studies includes programs in educational leadership; higher education and student affairs; history, philosophy, and policy education; and international and comparative education. Other areas of research and service are international educational reform, educational accessibility, program evaluations, and policy development. Departmental faculty work as partners with School of Education centers, the Indiana Urban Schools Association, and the Indiana Institute on Disability and Community. The department's Teacher Leader Pathway is a unique, fully online professional growth opportunity for classroom teachers seeking to acquire leadership skills or expand their impact on schools and districts.

The Department of Curriculum and Instruction has been reinforced by formerly independent departments, such as literacy, culture, and language education. The department sponsors 10 areas of concentration from art and science to mathematics and social science education. Rounding out its portfolio are teacher education and curriculum studies, early childhood education, and elementary and secondary education. Its teaching and research are extensive. One new research area is a peer-led teaming approach to globalizing rural science teacher preparation in the United States, funded by the Longview Foundation.

The Hybrid Secondary Transition to Teaching Program enrolls students with a bachelor's degree in a field other than teaching and is a pathway to licensure for those on an emergency license. The program offers a master's degree. The Office of Diversity, Equity, and Inclusion enhances community belonging of all students and provides professional development, community conversations, and social programs. The Global and International Engagement initiative supports international research and scholarship. It manages multiple, worldwide partnerships between the school and peer institutions.

These departments, offices, programs, services, and more can be accessed on the School of Education website (https://education.indiana.edu/). The internet is the future's gift to a history of the present. The School of Education website, however, was the gift of Ted Frick, former chair of IST, now professor emeritus. Frick said, "I created the virtual host name, https://education.indiana.edu, back in 1994. Maybe my most lasting contribution!"[110]

It is fitting this history concludes with a website, a distinct contrast to life in 1923. In the early 20th century, the School of Education moved from one building to the next, classes here, offices there. Now in the 21st century it moves at the speed of a keystroke across the world into homes and offices.

In degree but not in kind, the school that those visionary educational citizens began in 1923 is not that different from what the school is today: a literacy professor who devotes the last 10 years of her career to establishing higher education programs in Afghanistan for women and men to earn master's degrees; a young man who goes back to Spiceland, Indiana, to teach biology, still in touch with his high school chemistry teacher because "somebody's gotta lead the next generation"; a counselor who starts an extracurricular club for LGBTQ+ students in their high school in Bloomington; a graduate student who plays on a computer and invents an interactive video game to teach respect; a dean who says to two new faculty members, "Let's talk about how to fund that research project."

If education teaches a lesson, what is the lesson of the School of Education? What brought 10 students to the western edge of the wilderness to study Latin and Greek in Bloomington, Indiana, and go forth to teach? Why do faculty and staff, 200 years later, stay at their jobs for 40 or 50 years? One hopes this history suggests answers to these and other questions. History can only hint at the intangibles, however, and education has many of them—the inmost motives of teachers and counselors; life-changing sparks that illuminate classroom and clinic; organizational genius of servant leaders; showing up at the office for 50 years to help students graduate or teachers teach.

In 1927, not long after he handed the reins of the School of Education to Henry Lester Smith who would ride that horse for 30 years, President William Lowe Bryan published a little book of 17 pages, no bigger than a pocket Constitution. The book was *Paradise*. In it Bryan argued that when we take the long view of history, those who have suffered seem better off than those who came before. But when we look more closely, it is too soon to proclaim that all is right with the world. Consider the pardoned Jews of the Bible, he asked, or the liberated Blacks in 1865, or the warring nations on Armistice Day 1918 who proclaimed war is at end. They found Paradise. "Alas, it is hard to stay in Paradise," he wrote. Still, "it is possible to know the worst and *not* be a pessimist, to meet the worst without fear, without surrender." Without fear the scholar makes "not a new heaven but a new earth. In all these things our University, throughout its hundred years, has played its part." The trick (not Bryan's word) is to meet the worst and fight through it.

Consider "Booker Washington," Bryan wrote, "victim of race hatred from which there seems no escape— and he escapes. No man—I heard him say—no race shall degrade me by making me hate them." Or Lincoln "who faces the tragic years with grief but also with laughter, unbroken patience and unbroken will." Bryan asked, "Does not one of these win you to a banner of faith and of battle? Then, I show you a greater sight. I show you the countless multitude of *nameless* men and women who come up through the awful centuries covered with dust and blood but who never quite despair and who never surrender....Go up above them if you can—as far as you can—into the world of beauty and goodness...but you can never go high enough alone to reach Paradise."[111]

To approach Paradise, education goes high but not alone. It brings community. Those lovers of learning— the professor who risked her life in Afghanistan to educate women, the young man returning to Spiceland to lead the next generation, the counselor who held out a hand to trans and other sexual minorities, the graduate student who invented a game of respect—they do not go alone. They bear with them a community and history of classmates, colleagues, teachers, counselors, coaches, educational leaders. Whether they reach Paradise or not, what matters to them is a good day's work, a chance to make a difference, the privilege of responding to a call. Democracy is indebted to them.

After 100 years, what does the School of Education have to show for itself? There are many ways to assess it—quality of teaching, service, research; impact of graduates on society; impact of school on university. Each requires metrics. In the favorite phrase of a beloved education professor, one "quick and dirty" way to judge the school is to imagine the Spicelands and cities of Indiana without it. Given the history of the school, incomplete though it is, as an enduring yet mobile educational community of relationships—with others, with learning, with oneself, with technique—what would we have done without it?

# Author's Acknowledgments

Debts accumulate and I have many. Before this book was proposed to me, a cascade of events prepared my consent. I thank my husband, Don Maxwell, assistant professor of history, Indiana State University, who, four years ago, had the idea of a centennial symposium for Robert L. Gibson, my professor in the School of Education in 1980, who died at 95 in 2015, at whose centennial in 2019 I gave a paper that another professor of mine, Rex Stockton, heard and wanted me to do as a book for him, which I did, and that was read by my former School of Education colleagues Lynn Gilman and Joel Wong, who recommended me to Stacy Morrone, who asked me to do the same for the school's 100th anniversary, which I did, and which appears before you as this book. I am indebted to all of the above.

School of Education veteran faculty graciously allowed me to interview them or otherwise gave their support. They are Bob Arnove, Vic Borden, Barry Bull, Gary Crow, Lee Ehman, Ted Frick, Gerardo Gonzalez, Tom Gregory, Sam Guskin, Karen Hallett-Rupp, Jerry Harste, Gary Ingersoll, Susan Klein, Frank Lester, Mitzi Lewison, Marjorie Manifold, Terry Mason, Ed McClellan, Howard Mehlinger, Larry Mikulecky, Mike Molenda, Tom Schwen, Beau Vallance, Don Warren, Sue Whiston, and Enid Zimmerman. Jens Zorn, proud 92-year-old graduate of the University School and professor of physics emeritus, University of Michigan, granted me an interview. The knowledge and frank appraisals of these stalwarts made a better book, and I thank them all.

I must single out Don Warren and Ed McClellan. Don read the entire narrative except Chapter 5, which he felt uncomfortable commenting on because he was too close to its era. Ed read Chapters 3 and 5. Don and I exchanged detailed e-mails. He gave unstintingly of his vast expertise. I could not have hoped for more accomplished eyes on my narrative. I am humbled by the help of Don Warren and Ed McClellan. University Historian and Professor of History and Philosophy of Science and Medicine James H. Capshew read the first three chapters, for which I am grateful.

Others gave of their time and treasure: Valarie Akerson, Sarah Alexander, Elizabeth Boling, Curt Bonk, Gayle Buck, Doug Butler, Kate Cruikshank, Mary Dwyer, Ellen Haury, Maria Jensen, Christina Jones, Sherry Knighton-Schwandt, Chad Lochmiller, Chris Lubienski, Emily McCord, Lori Parker, Shirley Pugh, Charles Railsback, Charles Reafsnyder, Shawn Reynolds, Meredith Rogers, Pat (Mrs. John) Ryan, Patricia Scribner, Katie Smock, Laura Stachowski, Jesse Steinfeldt, Nancy Stockton, Vasti Torres, and Joel Wong.

Dina Kellams, director of University Archives, deserves special thanks. Reliable and efficient, Dina never faltered. She found everything I wanted and more. Gracious, detailed, timely, she brought history to life in box after box of letters, notes, memoranda, reports, drafts of speeches, pamphlets, and incunabula. Dina herself is an IU treasure. I thank her often.

Also assisting with history and documents were Christine Friesel, adult librarian and Indiana Room specialist, Monroe County Public Library; and Dan Clark, professor of history, Indiana State University (ISU) in Terre Haute. Christine's knowledge of Henry Lester Smith was essential to this book. She is a worthy guardian of his formidable legacy, for which I am appreciative. Dan Clark is author of *A History of Indiana State University: From Normal School to Teachers College, 1865–1933*. The histories of the IU School of Education and ISU intersect. Dan helped me learn about my school by talking about his. He alerted me to Christine Ogren's good critical history and historiography of teacher preparation in the United States. I thank him for these things and for his genial reception of me on his campus.

For books, journal and magazine articles, pamphlets, dissertation, blog, and chronologies, I have additional debts. Nina Krause gave me her copy of Herman Wells's *Being Lucky*, an excellent and well-written source of IU history. I relied on Marianne Mitchell's three-volume edition of Thomas D. Clark, *Indiana University: Midwestern Pioneer*; if only I could have thanked her in this life. Marianne's volume of J. Terry Clapacs, *Indiana University, Bloomington: America's Legacy Campus* was also helpful.

I benefited from other documents including *A Nation at Risk: The Imperative for Educational Reform*, A Report to the Nation and the Secretary of Education, United States Department of Education; John D. Barnhart & Donald F. Carmony, *Indiana: From Frontier to Industrial Commonwealth*, Vols. 1 & 2; Richard G. Boone, *A History of Education in Indiana*; William Lowe Bryan, "Address of Welcome" and *Paradise*;" David L. Clark, "Development– Responsibility of a Professional School;" Robert Joseph Elmes's dissertation, *Henry Lester Smith, Dean, School of Education, Indiana University 1916–1946*; Shirley H. Engle, "A Challenge to the School of Education and to Educators: Educational Technology and the Aims of Education"; and Eric Foner, *Give Me Liberty: An American History*, Vol. 2.

I learned from Laura Sheerin Gaus, *Shortridge High School: 1864–1981*; Hubert H. Hawkins, *Indiana's Road to Statehood: A Documentary Record*; Fred Hechinger, "Schoolyard Blues: The Decline of Public Education"; Herbert M. Kliebard, *The Struggle for the American Curriculum: 1893–1958*; William W. Lynch, "The Role of Research in Development"; James H. Madison, *The Indiana Way: A State History*, and *Hoosiers*; Velorus Martz, "The School of Education" in Burton Dorr Myers (ed. Ivy L. Chamness & Burton D. Myers), *History of Indiana University, Vol. II: The Bryan Administration (1902-1937)*; Howard D. Mehlinger, *The Best That I Can Recall*; Charles W. Moores, *Caleb Mills and the Indiana School System*; Patrick O'Meara, *Indiana University and the World: A Celebration of Collaboration, 1890-2018*; Jo Otremba's blog of January 27, 2023, "1930s Segregated Student Teaching and the IU Alumni Who Persevered (Part 1 of 3);" Mary Anne Raywid, Charles A. Tesconi, Jr., & Donald R. Warren, *Pride and Promise: Schools of Excellence for All the People*; and Henry Lester Smith, "The Underground Railroad in Monroe County."

Four School of Education publications were helpful: *Bulletin of the School of Education*; *Viewpoints: Bulletin of the School of Education* (the renamed *Bulletin*); *Chalkboard*; and the *Alumni Magazine* (the renamed *Chalkboard*). If you remain a work of education long enough, you are bound to be reinvented. Gelissia Honeycutt, executive assistant to dean after dean, wrote chronologies of the school that were useful springboards and helpful in themselves. In addition, I am grateful to three students, all of whom gave kindly of their time to be interviewed.

Finally, I thank my team: Dean Stacy Morrone for inviting me to write this book and for generous support throughout; Scott Witzke, media consultant, for his aesthetic genius and wide historical knowledge; and Chandler Hawkins, my graduate research assistant. I could not have written this book without Chandler. While preparing for and taking her qualifying exams, managing a dissertation proposal, and holding down another job, she was unfailing, unflinching, and unflappable. Chandler treated people with utmost respect. She located faculty and staff service records, deciphered state appropriations data, interpreted demographics on spreadsheets, attended meetings; she organized, interviewed, and wrote up observations; pursued the shy beast of enrollment data, suggested leads for research, kept in touch with sources until we got what we needed or gave up, located state licensure data, and worked well with her team members. Chandler has been a brilliant thinker, articulate witness, stellar citizen, and outstanding researcher. Her mark is everywhere in this book, as is my gratitude to her.

# Photo Credits

| | |
|---|---|
| iv | Image no. P0022535, Indiana University Archives |
| v | Image no. P0037591, Indiana University Archives |
| vii | Indiana Historical Bureau |
| 3 | Indiana University School of Education |
| 4 | *Left*: Image no. Image number: P0023077, Indiana University Archives |
| | *Right: I*mage No. P0023071, Indiana University Archives |
| 5 | *Top*: Image no. P0103029, Indiana University Archives |
| | *Bottom*: Image no. P0038133, Indiana University Archives |
| 10 | Image no. P0030754, Indiana University Archives |
| 11 | *Top:* Photo made from copy located in IU Libraries. Call number: L13 .I64 v.3 1926-1927 |
| | *Bottom:* Image no. P0111154, P0111156, P0111160, P0111161, P0111158, Indiana University Archives |
| 12 | Image no. P0023826, Indiana University Archives |
| 13 | Courtesy photo |
| 14 | Image no. P0023026, Indiana University Archives |
| 15 | *Left:* Image no. P0022459, Indiana University Archives |
| | *Right:* Image no. P0020915, Indiana University Archives |
| 16 | Image no. P0081284, Indiana University Archives |
| 18 | Image no. P0033242, Indiana University Archives |
| 19 | *Top:* Image no. P0052465, Indiana University Archives |
| | *Bottom:* Image no. P0112175, Indiana University Archives |
| 22 | Image no. P0112383, Indiana University Archives |
| 24 | Indiana University School of Education |
| 25 | *Left:* Indiana University School of Education |
| | *Right:* Image no. P0026433, Indiana University Archives |
| 26 | *Left and right:* Indiana University School of Education |
| 27 | *Left:* Image no. P0030518, Indiana University Archives |
| | *Right:* Image no. P0030520, Indiana University Archives |
| 28 | Image no. P0043346, Indiana University Archives |
| 30 | J. Scott Applewhite/AP |
| 31 | Image no. P0040173, Indiana University Archives |
| 32 | *Left:* Image no. P0112216, Indiana University Archives |
| | *Right:* Image no. P0112179, Indiana University Archives |
| 33 | Item 382-1362-043, IUPUI Image Collection |
| 35 | Image no. P0112382, Indiana University Archives |
| 37 | Image no. P0112385, Indiana University Archives |
| 38 | IU School of Education |
| 39 | Item UA024 PB07 0641, IUPUI Image Collection |

# Biographies

## Author

Frederic W. Lieber has Indiana roots. His great grandfather Richard Lieber founded the Indiana State Park system in 1916. His grandfather Clarence Efroymson was a freshman at IU in 1914, and IU President John Ryan conferred an honorary degree on him in 1985. His great uncle Lander MacClintock was professor of romance languages, later French and Italian, from 1920 to 1960. Frederic Lieber's family created the Frederic Bachman Lieber and Herman Frederic Lieber teaching awards at IU in the 1950s. He attended Shortridge High School in Indianapolis, the state's first free public high school.

Graduate of Brown University, Lieber received his doctorate from the IU Department of Counseling and Educational Psychology in 1995. He served as visiting assistant professor while working as a psychotherapist in private practice. He coordinated elementary teacher education in the School of Education and taught counseling, classroom management, history of psychology, and social psychology. For 12 years he taught courses in the history of ideas for Hutton Honors College. He is a poet and intellectual historian. He lives in Bloomington and is writing a history of empathy.

## Media Consultant

Scott Witzke has served as director of marketing and communications at the IU School of Education since January 2016. In 2018 he oversaw a complete redesign of the school's website. This task helped him gain a better understanding of the organizational structure of the school as well as how and where historical materials related to the school have been collected and archived. He would like to thank Bradley Cook in the IU Archives for his generous support in giving access to archival material as well as for locating and scanning many of the photos found in this publication. An alumnus of the Jacobs School of Music with a master's in lute performance, he previously served as marketing director at WFIU Public Radio and WTIU Public Television, and in the marketing department at the IU Credit Union.

## Research Assistant

Chandler Hawkins is a doctoral candidate in the Higher Education Program at Indiana University. She completed her undergraduate coursework at the University of Louisville majoring in public health and information sciences. During her undergraduate career, she developed a passion for advocacy in research, focusing much of her work on the importance of comprehensive sex education programs in the education setting. She then obtained a master of science in higher education and student affairs from Canisius College, completing a thesis on students of color's experiences during new-student orientation programs. Throughout her master's courses, she grounded her work in critical race theory and critiqued nuances in high impact practices and student development theory. She has expanded on her research in her doctoral career, as she has continued to implement a critical and transformative approach to research. Currently, her research focuses on the racialized and gendered experiences of Black undergraduate women, desirability, and sense of belonging. Primarily a qualitative researcher, she foregrounds Black feminist perspectives and seeks to continue amplifying the voices of those most marginalized.

# Notes

1   The quote is attributed to Mills in Laura Sheerin Gaus (1985). *Shortridge High School: 1864–1981*. Indianapolis: Indiana Historical Society, p.7. The words are inscribed above the proscenium arch in Caleb Mills Auditorium at Shortridge High School in Indianapolis, but the bibliographic source of the quote could not be located.

2   Hubert H. Hawkins (1969). Northwest Ordinance, 1787. *Indiana's Road to Statehood: A Documentary Record*. Indianapolis: Indiana Historical Bureau, p. 17.

3   Richard G. Boone (1892/1941). *A History of Education in Indiana*. New York: D. Appleton & Company (reprinted by the Indiana Historical Bureau), p. 360.

4   In 2017 the University had over 2,000 acres and 550 structures on the Bloomington campus. See J. Terry Clapacs (2017). *Indiana University, Bloomington: America's Legacy Campus*. Bloomington: Indiana University Press.

5   "Historical Sketch of the Schools" (1867). In *The Annual Report of the Public Schools of the City of Indianapolis for the School Year Ending Sept. 1, 1866*. Indianapolis: Douglass & Conner, Journal Office, Printers.

6   Thomas D. Clark (1970). *Indiana University: Midwestern Pioneer (Vol. I: The Early Years)*. Bloomington & London: Indiana University Press, p. 25.

7   Thomas D. Clark (1970). *Indiana University: Midwestern Pioneer (Vol. I: The Early Years)*. Bloomington & London: Indiana University Press, p. 83.

8   James H. Madison (1990). *The Indiana Way: A State History*. Bloomington & Indianapolis: Indiana University Press; and Indianapolis: Indiana Historical Society, p.113.

9   Charles W. Moores (1905). *Caleb Mills and the Indiana School System*. Indiana Historical Society Publications, Vol. III, No. VI. Indianapolis: The Wood-Weaver Printing Company.

10  Velorus Martz (1952). "The School of Education," in Burton Dorr Myers (eds. Ivy L. Chamness & Burton D. Myers), *History of Indiana University, Vol. II: The Bryan Administration (1902-1937)*. Bloomington: Indiana University, p. 592.

11  Monroe County History Center. "A 1904 History of Bloomington High School." https://monroehistory.org/2019/09/16/a-1904-history-of-bloomington-high-school/, accessed June 4, 2023.

12  Velorus Martz (1952). "The School of Education," in Burton Dorr Myers (eds. Ivy L. Chamness & Burton D. Myers), *History of Indiana University, Vol. II: The Bryan Administration (1902-1937)*. Bloomington: Indiana University, p. 556.

13  Thomas D. Clark (1973). *Indiana University: Midwestern Pioneer (Vol. II: In Mid-Passage)*. Bloomington & London: Indiana University Press, p. 243.

14  Herman B Wells (1980). *Being Lucky: Reminiscences & Reflections*. Bloomington & Indianapolis: Indiana University Press, p. 117.

15  Thomas D. Clark (1973). *Indiana University: Midwestern Pioneer (Vol. II: In Mid-Passage)*. Bloomington & London: Indiana University Press, p. xiii.

16  Robert Joseph Elmes (1969). *Henry Lester Smith, Dean, School of Education, Indiana University 1916–1946*. Unpublished doctoral dissertation, Indiana Room, Monroe County Public Library, Bloomington, Indiana, p. 59.

17  Patrick O'Meara (2019). *Indiana University and the World: A Celebration of Collaboration, 1890-2018*. Bloomington: Indiana University Press, p. 10.

18  Ibid.

19  Thomas D. Clark (1970). *Indiana University: Midwestern Pioneer (Vol. I: The Early Years)*. Bloomington & London: Indiana University Press, p. 296.

20  John D. Barnhart & Donald F. Carmony (1954). *From Frontier to Industrial Commonwealth*, Vol. 2. [1979 Reprint. Indianapolis: Indiana Historical Bureau]. Lewis Historical Publishing Co., p. 522.

21  Thomas D. Clark (1973). *Indiana University: Midwestern Pioneer (Vol. II: In Mid-Passage)*. Bloomington & London: Indiana University Press, p. 246.

22  "President's Report to the Honorable Board of Trustees of Indiana University" (October 30, 1922). Box 9. IU Archives. Bloomington, Indiana.

23  Henry Lester Smith (1917). "The Underground Railroad in Monroe County," *Indiana Magazine of History*, vol. 13, no. 3, September, pp. 288–297.

24  Robert Joseph Elmes (1969). *Henry Lester Smith, Dean, School of Education, Indiana University, 1916-1946*. Unpublished doctoral dissertation, Indiana Room, Monroe County Public Library, Bloomington, Indiana, p. 50.

25  Jo Otremba (January 27, 2023). "1930s Segregated Student Teaching and the IU Alumni Who Persevered" (Part 1 of 3). https://blogs.libraries.indiana.edu/iubarchives/2023/01/27/1930s-segregated-student-teaching-part-1/, accessed April 17, 2023.

26  Velorus Martz (1952). "The School of Education," in Burton Dorr Myers (eds. Ivy L. Chamness & Burton D. Myers), *History of Indiana University, Vol. II: The Bryan Administration (1902-1937)*. Bloomington: Indiana University, p. 571.

27  Jens Zorn, personal communication, April 16, 2023.

28  Thomas Schwen, personal communication, May 18, 2023.

29  The train story comes from Michael Molenda, personal communication, February 3, 2023.

30  Thomas D. Clark (1977). *Indiana University: Midwestern Pioneer (Vol. III: Years of Fulfillment)*. Bloomington & London: Indiana University Press, p. 35.

31  Herman B Wells (1980). *Being Lucky: Reminiscences & Reflections.* Bloomington & Indianapolis: Indiana University Press, p. 260.

32  Oscar O. Winther & Thomas D. Clark (1968). *Oral History Interview with Lander MacClintock.* IU Archives. Bloomington, Indiana, pp. 14-15. MacClintock is the great-uncle of the author of the current book, proof that blood devises no laws for the brain.

33  Robert Joseph Elmes (1969). *Henry Lester Smith, Dean, School of Education, Indiana University, 1916-1946.* Unpublished doctoral dissertation, Indiana Room, Monroe County Public Library, Bloomington, Indiana, p. 66.

34  "School of Education Building 1951." C110 Box 12. IU Archives. Bloomington, Indiana.

35  "Minutes of the Committee of Teacher Education," October 6, 1952. Box 2018/066.17. IU Archives. Bloomington, Indiana.

36  "Register of Research Centers, Institutes, and Museums—IUB." Box 2018/066, IU Archives. Bloomington, Indiana.

37  David L. Clark (1993). "Former Deans of Education Reflect on School's Past," *Chalkboard*, Spring/Summer, p. 22.

38  Samuel Guskin, personal communication, March 2023.

39  David L. Clark (1970). "Development – Responsibility of a Professional School." *Viewpoints: Bulletin of the School of Education* vol. 46, no. 2, March, pp. 1–2.

40  "Reorganization of Teacher Education." Box 2018/066.16, p. 70. IU Archives. Bloomington, Indiana.

41  "Reorganization." Box 2018/066.16, p. 1. IU Archives. Bloomington, Indiana.

42  Thomas D. Clark (1977). *Indiana University: Midwestern Pioneer (Vol III: Years of Fulfillment)*. Bloomington & London: Indiana University Press, p. 617.

43  Herman Wells considered Ryan's organization of regional campuses "brilliantly achieved," and his international work exemplary [Herman B Wells (1980). *Being Lucky: Reminiscences & Reflections.* Bloomington & Indianapolis: Indiana University Press, pp. 119, 253)].

44  Herman B Wells (January 21, 1970). *Viewpoints: Bulletin of the School of Education* vol. 46, no. 2, March, p. 8.

45  William W. Lynch (1970). "The Role of Research in Development." *Viewpoints: Bulletin of the School of Education* vol, 46, no. 2, March, p. 18.

46  US Department of Education (April 1983). *A Nation at Risk: The Imperative for Educational Reform.* A Report to the Nation and the Secretary of Education by The National Commission on Excellence in Education. Washington, D.C., p. 5.

47  Howard D. Mehlinger (2009). *The Best That I Can Recall.* Bloomington: AuthorHouse, p. 299.

48  Ibid., p. 300.

49  Howard D. Mehlinger, personal communication, December 20, 2022.

50  "Task Force on Trends in Federal Support for Higher Education—Final Report." Indiana University Bloomington Faculty Council Circular. B07-1978. IU Archives. Bloomington, Indiana.

51  "Register of Research Centers, Institutes, & Museums." Box 2018/C6610, IU Archives. Indiana University, Bloomington, Indiana.

52  Samuel Guskin, personal communication, May 8, 2023.

53  Fred Hechinger (1979). "Schoolyard Blues: The Decline of Public Education." *Saturday Review*, vol. 6, no. 2, pp. 20–22.

54  "School of Education Center for Excellence—Beginnings 1983." Box 2018/066.10. IU Archives. Bloomington, Indiana.

55  Howard Mehlinger, personal communication, December 20, 2022.

56  The central thrust of such reforms was set forth in *Tomorrow's Teachers: A Report of the Holmes Group*, published by The Holmes Group (East Lansing: Michigan State University), 1986. The group was a consortium of education deans and chief academic officers of American research universities, chaired by Judith E. Lanier, dean of the College of Education, Michigan State University.

57  "School of Education Center for Excellence in Education–Beginnings 1983." Box 2018/066.10, IU Archives. Bloomington, Indiana.

58  "Consortium on Education Policy Studies." Box 2018/066.15. IU Archives. Bloomington, Indiana.

59  Barry Bull, personal communication, January 26, 2023.

60  "COTEP September 1986," pp. 1, 2, 73. Box 2018/066.12. IU Archives. Bloomington, Indiana.

61  Howard Mehlinger (2009). *The Best That I Can Recall*. Bloomington, IN: AuthorHouse, p. 332.

62  Donald Warren (1990). "Dean's Comments." *Chalkboard*, Fall/Winter, p. 2.

63  Donald Warren, personal communication, January 17, 2023.

64  The quote comes from "Historical Sketch of the Schools," in *The Annual Report of the Public Schools of the City of Indianapolis for the School Year Ending Sept. 1, 1866.* (Indianapolis: Douglass & Conner, Journal Office, Printers, 1867. Quoted in Laura Sheerin Gaus (1985), *Shortridge High School: 1864–1981*. Indianapolis: Indiana Historical Society, p. 6.

65  J. Terry Clapacs (2017). *Indiana University, Bloomington: America's Legacy Campus*. Bloomington: Indiana University Press, pp. 169, 171.

66  Richard G. Boone (1892). *A History of Education in Indiana*. New York: D. Appleton & Company. Reprinted by the Indiana Historical Bureau, Indianapolis, 1941, p. 354; and Thomas D. Clark (1970). *Indiana University: Midwestern Pioneer (Vol. I: The Early Years)*. Bloomington and Indianapolis: Indiana University Press, p. 31.

67  Personal interview, April 24, 2023.

68  Donald Warren (1990). "Dean's Comments." *Chalkboard*, Fall/Winter, p. 2.

69  Donald Warren (1991). "Dean's Comments." *Chalkboard*, Fall/Winter, p. 1.

70  Donald Warren, personal interview, April 24, 2023.

71  William Lowe Bryan (1923). "Address of Welcome." Proceedings of the High School Principals' Conference, Held at Indiana University, November 23-24, 1923, Under the Auspices of the School of Education, Indiana University. *Bulletin of the School of Education* vol. 1, no. 1, p. 3.

72  Ibid.

73  Donald Warren (1993). "Dean's Comments." *Chalkboard*, Spring/Summer, p. 2.

74  Martha McCarthy (1992). "Martha McCarthy Issues Warning: Censorship is Growing." *Chalkboard*, Spring/Summer, p. 4.

75  Donald Warren (1993). "Nebraska Cropsey and the Imperative of Educational Purpose." *Chalkboard*, Spring/Summer, p. 1.

76  Ibid.

77  Consistent institutional evidence of gender, race/ethnicity, and economic status is difficult to find. The best estimate is that Warren hired 30 female faculty out of a total of 45 hires during his tenure.

78  Shirley H. Engle (1993). "A Challenge to the School of Education and to Educators: Educational Technology and the Aims of Education." *Chalkboard*, Fall/Winter, p. 2.

79  Ellen Haury, personal communication, May 10, 2023.

80  Susan Klein, personal communication, May 12, 2023.

81  Ibid.

82  Tom Gregory, personal communication, March 27, 2023.

83  Tom Gregory (1990). "Toby May: A Tragic Day in the Life of Mountain Open High School." *Chalkboard*, Fall/Winter, pp. 8–10.

84  Ibid.

85  Ibid.

86  Ibid.

87  Barry Bull, personal communication, January 26, 2023.

88  Gerardo Gonzalez, personal communication, January 30, 2023.

89  Indiana Developmental and Content Standards for Educators, Final Report (December 2010). Indiana Department of Education.

90  Gerardo Gonzalez, personal communication, January 30, 2023.

91  Gerardo Gonzalez (2001). "The Dean's Perspective." *Chalkboard*, Spring/Summer, p. 1.

92  *Draft of School of Education Long-Range Strategic Plan*, May 1, 2002, prepared by Long-Range Planning Committee, Charles M. Reigeluth, Chair (Indiana University Bloomington).

93  Gerardo Gonzalez (2005). "The Dean's Perspective." *Chalkboard*, Spring/Summer, p. 1.

94   Ellen Brantlinger (2004). "Special Education Professor Works to Break Down Barriers Dividing Classes." *Chalkboard*, Spring/Summer, p. 4.

95   "News Briefs" (2006–2007). *Chalkboard*, Fall/Winter, p. 5.

96   Eric Foner (2012). *Give Me Liberty: An American History* (Vol. 2, Seagull Third ed.) New York: W.W. Norton & Co., pp. 1146–1148.

97   Gerardo Gonzalez (2014). "Letter to Editor." *IndyStar*, November 4.

98   *News at IU*/Indiana University, August 11, 2017.

99   Terrence Craig Mason (2015). *Important Message about the School of Education Dean Search.* Electronic mail. December 10, 2015.

100 Keith Barton (2020). "Terrence C. Mason." *In Honor of Retiring Faculty.* Indiana University, p. 38.

101 Terrence Craig Mason, personal communications, December 29, 30, 2022.

102 Lemuel Watson (2018). "Dean's Perspective." *Chalkboard*, Spring, p. 1.

103 Personal communication, spring 2023.

104 "Anastasia Morrone Named Interim Dean of the School of Education in Bloomington, July 7, 2020." *News at IU*. Indiana University.

105 Ibid.

106 Anastasia Morrone (2020–2021). "Dean's Perspective." *School of Education Alumni Magazine*, Winter, p. 3.

107 Ibid.

108 Suzanne Eckes, personal communication, summer 2021.

109 Frederic W. Lieber (2019). "From Deeper Teaching to Wider Guidance: Robert L. Gibson and the Postwar Expansion of Student Services in the United States." Paper presented at the Robert L. Gibson Centennial Symposium, School of Education, Indiana University, Bloomington, Indiana, October 19, 2019, pp. 1–2.

110 Ted Frick, personal communication, April 1, 2023.

111 William Lowe Bryan (1927). *Paradise*. Bloomington, Indiana: Indiana University Bookstore.

Printed in the United States
by Baker & Taylor Publisher Services